Affinographs

Davor Jedlicka

Affinographs

A Dynamic Method for Assessment of Individuals, Couples, Families, and Households

Springer

Davor Jedlicka Ph.D.
Department of Social Sciences
The University of Texas at Tyler
3900 University Blvd.
Tyler, TX 75799
USA
davor1945@gmail.com

ISBN 978-1-4419-9394-6 e-ISBN 978-1-4419-9395-3
DOI 10.1007/978-1-4419-9395-3
Springer New York Dordrecht Heidelberg London

Library of Congress Control Number: 2011927936

Printed on acid-free paper

Springer is part of Springer Science+Business Media (www.springer.com)

To Linton C. Freeman

Foreword to Davor Jedlicka's *Affinographs*

I am so pleased to see Davor Jedlicka's *Affinographs* made available to those from many disciplines who will benefit from his methodological innovation that I believe to have theoretical consequences as well.

As an anthropologist interested in the use of network models to "understand human form and behavior and the varieties thereof," as the founder of American anthropology described the purpose of our science, I have long felt that our ways of visualizing and charting kinship and other human institutions put too much emphasis on the persons and paid insufficient attention to the relations among them.

From a holistic perspective, AHA! moments of understanding in the sciences occur only once we have adjusted our techniques so that we focus on relations rather than things themselves. We may not fully understand physics, but certainly recognizing the *relativism* among the things we observe seems necessary to the gains we have made. You cannot fully understand the *elements* until you see them as *components* within a dynamic system. In biology as well, our understanding depends more on our learning about the relations among organisms and species than it does upon descriptions of each separately.

In anthropology we used to speak of cultural traits being invented and diffused. Human culture made little sense—a thing of shreds and patches—until we perceived that our observations were integrated into dynamic cultural systems. Only then, when we saw how observed behaviors are logically related, could culture be understandable, the whole being recognized as more than the sum of its parts.

In an ethnographic kinship chart, the kin terms and their connecting lines are little more than words and lines until we grasp the meaning of those relationships. Levi-Strauss gave us a structural boost when he focused on the relations and declared that certain relations—the mother–child relation, the father–child relation, the sibling relation, and the relation between the mother's brother and sister's son—formed the *elementary structure of kinship* for human beings. The relations among the relations are as crucial to the system as the nodes themselves.

Davor Jedlicka's *affinographs* offers a way to chart the related lives of many people in all kinds of human communities. With his graph theoretic background, he developed a way to put together the different kinds of networks—networks of people and networks of relationships in one graph.

I have followed with considerable interest and admiration Davor Jedlicka's pioneering work in developing techniques of representing family, household, and kinship relationships currently and through time and generations. His *affinograph* representation is far superior to the traditional techniques of kinship charting that have been the mainstay of anthropology, sociology, and social work for more than a hundred years.

What is truly exciting is that *affinographs* can be applied much more broadly in social network analyses in all kinds of interpersonal and interorganizational systems.

Distinguished Professor Emeritus, Anthropology Alvin Wolfe
University of South Florida

Preface

This book has been evolving since I took my first class with Linton C. Freeman at the University of Hawaii in 1972. In Professor Freeman's course on Mathematical Models in Sociology, I wrote a paper using relations rather than persons in a study of marriage, divorce, and remarriage. In December of 1974, at the University of Hawaii, Forest Pitts, professor of geography and Linton Freeman, professor of sociology, organized a Social Networks Colloquium. At that same colloquium in 1975, I presented a paper entitled "Serial Marriage Networks: A Study of Change in the American Family" (Jedlicka 1975b).

Two years later, I was honored with an invitation by Dr. Freeman to be one of forty social scientists in his study sponsored by the National Science Foundation "to test the effectiveness of a new computer-based communications system" (Freeman 2004, p. 151). The project began with an in-person meeting in January of 1978. Alvin Wolfe, professor of anthropology at the University of South Florida, attended the meeting. Dr. Wolfe's enthusiasm for *network thinking* encouraged me to pursue the network notions in the study of family relations.

Most research on family networks in anthropology and sociology has never crossed into counseling, family therapy, and social work. To gain a perspective of the applied behavioral and social sciences, I went back to school to study family therapy. In 1999, I received a doctorate in that field from the Texas Woman's University in Denton, Texas.

During the annual meeting of the International Network for Social Network Analysis held in Vancouver, Canada in the year 2000, I presented a paper entitled "The Use of Genographs in Family Assessment of Serial Monogamy" (Jedlicka 2000). At that conference, Alvin Wolfe gave some useful feedback regarding genograph representations of children. For five years after that conference, I experimented with methods for representing children in reference to their custodial and birth parents. The difficulty was with accounting for children whose parents moved from household to household with a different partner. After many trials, I settled on a straightforward system for tracking children from birth through the most recent residence.

Once I could graphically track children over time, I realized that the word *genograph* closely resembled the well-established, static technique called *genogram*.

From the title of Lewis Henry Morgan's book *Systems of Consanguinity and Affinity of the Human Family*, I used the word *affinity* to coin the word *affinograph*. The new word departs from the *geno* stem of the genogram and identifies the *graph* as a mathematical basis for the model.

Affinographs were developed through my marriage and the family classes, and through my observations as an intern in various mental health clinics. Over the years, I have followed the strictest ethical standards while testing affinographs. Students in my classes have never been coerced by grade or extra credit or any other means of coercion to use an affinograph on their own families. Students always had an option of using examples of family narratives I provided if they did not wish to use their own families as examples.

Some case studies used in this book are based on my clinical experience as a supervised intern. Over seven years, I worked under supervision in a psychiatric clinic, two family counseling clinics, home counseling program, brain injury clinic, and a shelter for abandoned children. All clients observed in this study had signed informed consents with the understanding that their case will be used confidentially for education and research. I changed names, places, and sometimes family constellations to assure that no one could be identified.

In addition to Linton C. Freeman and Alvin W. Wolfe, my gratitude also goes to Glen Jennings, professor of family sciences at Texas Woman's University. For eight years, Dr. Jennings helped me gain the clinical experience necessary to write *Affinographs*. I am grateful to my wife Barbara who helped me develop a general definition of the family. I am also grateful to Maggie Haas for preparing most of the figures in this book, to my colleague Dr. Dana Adams for his editing of the manuscript, and to Kenisha Schuster for editing the cited references. Furthermore, many thanks to Charlotte Chambers of the Department of Social Sciences at the University of Texas at Tyler for many years of providing competent and dependable technical and administrative support.

Professor of Sociology at the University of Texas at Tyler

Davor Jedlicka
Ph.D., LMFT

Contents

List of Figures

Chapter 1
What Is an Affinograph?

Abstract An affinograph is a dynamic graph image of family relationships accumulated through descent, civil unions, informal unions, marriage, procreation, and adoption. An affinograph gives a more precise meaning to families referred to as broken, nuclear, reconstituted, blended, single-parent, and others. Affinographs transfer descriptive narratives of family relations into images that help generate working hypotheses for clinical interventions, teaching, and research. Five assumptions underlie affinograph images: One, affinal relations vary from ephemeral to life long. Two, each adult may remain eligible to start a new relationship regardless of the current marital status. Three, families can be formed with or without marriage. Four, relationship commitment is gender neutral. And five, a person may have more than two parents.

An affinograph is a model for imaging family relationships accumulated through any combination of descent, civil unions, informal unions, marriage, procreation, and adoption. This definition meets four criteria of Freeman's paradigm for social science research in general. One, it is amenable to social network analysis. Two, it requires systemic data. Three, it can be graphically represented (Freeman 2000). And four, its graphical representations are mathematically rigorous (Freeman 2004, p. 3).

The affinographs are related to what is called in *social network analysis* "affiliation networks" (Wasserman and Faust 2009, pp. 291–343). Affinographs can be viewed as a subset of affiliation networks in that they share some common properties. Both affinographs and affiliation networks are two-mode networks with one set of actors. The first mode represents actors, and the second mode is a set of events. The affiliation networks encompass a broad range of events such as belonging to clubs, organizations, belonging to cliques, and so on (Knoke and Yang 2008, pp. 103–117). An affiliation network can also represent a cohort (Jedlicka 1975a). Affinographs, on the other hand, focus on a subset of events relating to *affinity and consanguinity.*

The word *affinograph* is a compound of the words *affinity* and *graph.* The word *affinity* includes all intimate relations from the most ephemeral to the most com-

D. Jedlicka, *Affinographs,* DOI 10.1007/978-1-4419-9395-3_1,

mitted. Affinal relations can be discerned from a variety of sources, including interviews, expert assessment, historical documents, and narratives. In clinical applications, the decision of whether or not a relation belongs in an affinograph depends on the client's perception. Even an ephemeral relation can influence a person's current relations in some instances. Hence, clients decide what a relationship means to them.

The word *graph* signifies a close relationship between the graph theory and affinal networks. I will use the word *graph* to refer to the mathematical structures and the word *network* to refer to the social structures, which the graphs represent. The graph theory is essential for the understanding of the origin of the affinograph, but it is not necessary to know the graph theory to apply affinographs. The mathematical underpinnings provide the necessary rigor to define an affinograph as a graphic model.

Affinographs can also be defined according to what they do: generate hypotheses and heuristic ideas for applications in research, teaching, and clinical settings. Let me then stipulate that an affinograph is a graph model, a family image, and a hypothesis generator. Even though these definitions together constitute the affinograph method of analysis, each has a different focus and different applications. Because the graph theory is the basis of all affinograph applications, it is befitting to begin with the discussion of an affinograph as a graph model.

An Affinograph Is a Graph Model of Serial Relations

Like so many other terms in sociology, *model* has many meanings and many functions (Apostel 1961). Graph models embody social network notions, which can generate heuristic ideas (Busacker and Saaty 1965; Freeman 2004; Harary 1972; Wilson and Watkins 1990). An affinograph is a cognitive model when it portrays perceived relationships from the ego's perspective. In Farber's words, affinographs would be a model of "cognitive kinship maps" (Farber 1981, p. 45).

A graph model includes persons and relations between them. In a graph, a population set P contains of persons u:

$$P = \{u|u \text{ is a person}\}.$$

The second required set of a graph model contains relations. A relation R stands for any pair in the set P as follows:

$$R = \{\langle u, v\rangle \text{ person u is in a relation with person v}\}.$$

The canonical form, which is the simplest standard form of family relationships data, is an ordered pair $S=\{P, R\}$, which can also be expressed as a graph G, such as

$$G = \langle P', R'\rangle \text{ and the set}$$
$$P' = \{u'|u' \text{ is a point}\}.$$

Directed lines between members of the set P′ form a set of relations R′ such that

$$R' = \{\langle u', v' \rangle \mid \text{there is a directed line from } u' \text{ to } v'\}.$$

A graph model requires a set of two or more points and the lines connecting them (Taylor 1970, p. 51). The conventional images of family structures use points or geometric figures to represent people and lines between these symbols to represent relationships. In an affinograph, points represent relationships and lines represent people who add or change relationships. This reversal is a procedure known as *condensation.*

An affinograph of condensed points constitutes what Harary and Batell (1981) call *a level-2 network* and Wolfe (1978) calls *relations among relations.* A level-2 network diminishes representational problems in serial monogamy, polygamy, and families with diverse relationships. Harary et al. (1965, p. 59) define condensation as an operation that allows representation of a set of people with a point. The people are partitioned into disjoint, nonempty subsets whose union is all of that set. At some point in time, the condensed pairs are disjoint: There is a unique "u" and "v" comprising only one pair. Pairs can be of the same or different genders; additionally, the relationship status does not enter into the partitioning process. In other words, the basis of an affinograph is a representational technique that uses points to represent relations, families, and households. Lines represent people who change their relationships or add new ones.

With the passage of time, some pairs dissolve and new ones may join with the old. For example, a child leaving home to marry remains in a relationship with his or her parents while forming new relations with people originally outside of the family. In a joint relation, a person is a part of more than one pair. An affinograph model tracks the history of relations terminated by deaths, divorces, and separation, reflecting the dynamics of a family structure.

An Affinograph Is a Dynamic Model

An affinograph is a dynamic model, because it represents relationships by time sequences rather than by location of symbols on a page. Genograms, family trees, and family diagrams rely on the relative location of symbols, usually top and bottom or left and right, to indicate a sequence or a temporal order. Such conventions preclude applications of the graph theory for social network analysis. In contrast, an affinograph complies with the graph theory in that the beginning and the end point of a line indicate the time sequence regardless of the relative location of points.

Chapter 3 shows in some detail how to use points and lines to represent the past and present relationships in an affinograph. Lines in an affinograph connect relationships thus adding time as a representational dimension of the graph theory. Graph theory conventions identify links from generation to generation and changes in relationships as they occur within a same generation.

Even though relations are condensed into points, the identity of each person in the network can be preserved through *partitioning.* An affinograph partitions each population into two mutually exclusive subsets. Every person in an affinograph can be associated at birth with parents. With time, most people form relationships outside of the family of origin. An affinograph distinguishes those who form new relationships from those who do not. This partitioning is a key to the affinograph parsimony. There is no need for geometric symbols to represent people who have never formed affinal relationships. Chapter 3 shows how condensation provides parsimony without sacrificing details found in static models.

In general, relationships represented in affinographs are classified according to the following rules:

1. *The number of points in a graph is finite and greater than 0.* Regardless of who defines a family, each family has its boundary.
2. *The number of lines is finite and can be equal to 0.* Because lines represent people who move from one relationship to another, the highest number of lines emanating from any one point is limited by the number of people in the initial relationship. If no one forms a new relationship, there are no lines.
3. *The maximum number of lines associated with a point is equal to the number of people represented by a condensed point.* A condensed point usually represents parents and their children. If parents divorced and each remarried, and all of their children married, the number of lines emanating from the condensed point would be equal to the number of children plus one line for each parent.
4. *Each line originates from a point and terminates in a point.* A line represents a person moving from one relationship to another. The point of destination of a line is called a *vertex.* Each vertex in an affinograph is a relation in discrete time.
5. *There are no loops.* A loop would indicate a relation with oneself.
6. *There can be parallel lines.* A parallel line designates a breakup of a relationship followed by the reconciliation. In Chap. 9, this case is illustrated with the two consecutive marriages in a series of marriages by Elizabeth Taylor and Richard Burton.

Theoretically, there is a high limit on how many times a person can form a new relationship. The New York Times, January 30, 1984 reported that Glynn Wolfe "takes 26th wife." At that time, he was 75 years old and remarried three more times before his death at age 89. Even in this extreme example, one person's experience is not enough to ascertain the complexity of a family. The complexity of the family structure can expand through the network of each person involved even after two consecutive relationships. An image of such a complex family narrative is indeed worth a thousand words.

An Affinograph Is an Image of a Family Narrative

An affinograph can be viewed as an image of a narrative description of a family. In clinical settings, affinographs are used when notes alone may be difficult to use for tracking, interpreting, assessing, and helping a family to change (Sprenkle and

Fisher 1978). To comprehend the intertwined relationships described in narratives, Chaps. 4–8 convert narratives into parsimonious images. Chapter 4 suggests that images can help social workers track and locate children entrusted to their oversight.

Chapter 5 converts narratives of sequences of marriages and divorces into networks of relationships across several households. In this chapter, affinographs provide precise images of terms like *nuclear family, single-parent family, broken family, reconstituted family, blended family*, and others. The collective term proposed in Chap. 5 for families formed through serial monogamy is *compound family*.

Compound families can include same-gender couples. Chapter 6 focuses on imaging some common narratives relating to same-gender families. Subjects in research or clients in clinical and service settings provide the meaning of these images. Chapter 7 examines the narratives of extramarital affairs and ephemeral relations and puts them into the context of the larger family system.

Family therapists who use genograms are trained to deal with family systems (Congress 1994; Hardy and Laszloffy 1995; Hodge 2005; McGill 1992; Rigazio-DiGilio et al. 2005; Roberto 1992; Thomas 1998). Systemic therapists can combine affinographs with genograms to assist them in collaboration with their clients to generate clinical hypotheses.

An Affinograph Is a Hypotheses-Generating Model

Chapter 8 explores the use of affinographs for hypotheses formation and interventions in family therapy. The predictive interpretations of affinographs are explored using case studies. Case studies show that affinographs may provide clues about the effect of family structure on the emotional well-being of clients as suggested by Bernard (1956) more than half a century ago. Bernard found that when one ex-spouse remarries and the other does not, the one that remains unmarried is likely to interfere with the ex-spouse's new marriage (Bernard 1956, pp. 202–205). At about the same time, Bott (1957) generated a hypothesis linking the network structure with the role-relationship between husband and wife: "The degree of segregation in the role-relationship of husband and wife varies directly with the connectedness of the family's social network" (Bott 1957, p. 60).

Since the 1950s, formal models used for generating hypotheses in family research abound (Foster and Seidman 1992; Harary and Batell 1981; Harary and White 2001; Levi-Strauss 1949/1969; Ore 1960; White 2004; White et al. 1999). Harary and White (2001) described a model they called *p-graph* to image kinship and marriage ties. The p-graphs share characteristics with genograms and affinographs. For example, a vertex in a p-graph and an affinograph can represent relationships within families, business, or other organizations. However, another vertex in the p-graph corresponds to the geometric symbols used to represent persons in genograms. Such complex conventions of representation render the p-graphs and other formal models referenced above unsuited for use in clinical settings.

Less formal models designed for applications in clinical settings tend to disregard mathematical axioms entirely. Affinographs, on the other hand, rely on the graph-theory axioms. These axioms underlie the assumptions, which form the framework for clinical and pedagogical applications of the affinograph.

Assumptions Underlying Affinographs

Each representational model embodies a set of assumptions. The affinograph assumptions are based on a key social constructionist principle: Clients are experts on defining their own family boundaries and on defining the meaning of their own relationships (Widmer and La Farga 1999; Freeman and Couchonnal 2006). The affinograph assumptions also conform to the axioms of the graph theory across the range of family systems around the world.

Assumption 1. *Affinal relations vary from ephemeral to life long.* This assumption recognizes that even a brief, intimate relation can have a lasting influence on the individual and family. An ephemeral sexual encounter, for example, may result in a pregnancy, disease, or a hard-to-break emotional attachment. Given the frailty of some people to cope with the past, one should not dismiss relations simply because they were brief or did not produce children, disease, or lasting commitment. If a relation of any duration is significant to the ego, it can be visualized in an affinograph.

Assumption 2. *Married people may remain available for life in the field of those eligible to form a relationship.* This assumption brings to focus the porous boundary of marriage. A pair, married or not, with or without children, may break or add relationships at any time. In the United States, by age sixty, about 42% of men and about 40% of women have been divorced at least once (U.S. Census Bureau 2001, Table 1). Most of those who divorced remarried and became a part of a social network consisting of expartners, children, siblings, half siblings, and other relations.

Assumption 3. *Families are formed with or without marriage.* A person may have a child without marriage. Some families consist of networks of parents and children distributed among several households without anyone in two or more generations ever being married.

Assumption 4. *Relationship commitment is gender neutral.* An affinograph represents relations without a gender bias, because those involved in relationships define their own level of commitment and the nature of their union regardless of cultural, institutional, or observer views toward gender.

Assumption 5. *Each person has as many parents as that person identifies through experience.* This assumption takes into account that just one remarriage for each parent establishes a family of four parents. For some children, each of these parents serves as an object of attachment. An affinograph represents these parents as a part of the family network with roles and functions of each parent defined from the point of view of the child.

These assumptions also apply to genealogical methods, including the images known as family trees. Chapter 9 illustrates the use of affinographs in some challenging cases of family trees with meandering roots.

Chapter 2
Why Affinographs?

Abstract One reason to consider affinographs is that graphic imaging methods have not kept pace with the changing family forms. An affinograph is an interdisciplinary method for imaging the dynamic family systems across cultures. The affinograph images are distinguished from other imaging methods in that they relate to a general definition of the human family system. In addition to imaging the static family structures, an affinograph provides images of relationships that accumulate through descent and affinal unions such as marriage, remarriage, civil unions, or informal unions. Affinographs could be applied in social work, counseling, family therapy, and in family science teaching and research in general.

The fundamental rationale for "why affinographs" is the same as the rationale Lewis Henry Morgan provided for his systemic, graphic imagery of "Consanguinity and Affinity of the Human Family" (Morgan 1870/1997). Morgan proposed the use of images to "ascertain differences and typical forms of general family systems" (p. 7). In the nineteenth century, the family systems were predominantly stable and predictable. Since then, American families have become more diverse, less predictable, and predominantly serial rather than monogamous and stable (Starbuck 2010, p. 268; Cherlin 2005). By age 45, more than half of American men have had eight or more partners and more than half of American women have had four or more partners (Mosher et al. 2005). Accompanying this trend is "the increasing number of cohabiting unions and the emergence of same-sex marriage" (Cherlin 2004). The currently promoted imaging methods for applications in family life education and in clinical settings have not kept pace with the changing family forms. Therefore, affinographs are proposed as an alternative imaging method in applications dealing with diverse, complex, and dynamic families.

The affinograph is not the only dynamic model for family imaging. Anthropologists and mathematical sociologists have developed formal, dynamic models for imaging family relationships (Howell 1988; Klovdahl 1981; Levi-Strauss 1949/1969; Tjon Sie Fat 1983; Wellman 1988; White 2004; White et al. 1999; White and Jorion 1992; White and Reitz 1983). The affinograph is still needed, because formal models tend to be complicated and impractical. None of the formal models has been designed for clinical applications. In applied settings, family imaging has been limited

D. Jedlicka, *Affinographs,* DOI 10.1007/978-1-4419-9395-3_2,

to the use of static models only, such as genograms (DeMaria et al. 1999; Marlin 1989; McGoldrick and Gerson 1985; McGoldrick et al. 1999), family maps (Goldenberg and Goldenberg 2008, pp. 192–194; Mattaini 1997), and family diagrams (Bradt 1980; Butler 2008).

In general, applications of static models in family counseling and therapy tend to be restricted to the immediate family members (Carvalho et al. 2008; Coco and Courtney 2003; Duba et al. 2009; Eichholz 2003; Kelly 2003; Lewis 1989; Lim and Nakamoto 2008; Massey et al. 1988; Nichols and Schwartz 2006, p. 89; Worden 2003, p. 109).

Some forms of counseling such as spiritual counseling (Hodge 2001, 2005), child welfare practice (McMillen and Groze 1994), and individual counseling (Daughhetee 2001) also tend to exclude family members beyond those immediately involved in counseling. Even group counseling (Davis et al. 1988) seems to restrict genograms to the immediate family members. Health professionals (Like et al. 1988; Tomson 1985; Waters et al. 1994; Werner-Lin 2007) and educators (Howell 1988; Shellenberger et al. 2007; Willow et al. 2009) also tend to isolate the family of origin and family of procreation. Given that the "intimate psychological network" typically includes about twenty five people (Pattison et al. 1979), the affinograph is suggested as a method for imaging more complex family constellations.

There appears to be a niche for applications of genograms and affinographs. For example, in my family classes I introduce students to genograms and affinographs as two versions of family diagrams. I then ask them if they have no objection to choose one or the other to diagram their own family. An overwhelming number of students with divorces and remarriages in their own families choose to use affinographs. Those with intact families tend to choose genograms. I anticipate that clinicians would make the same choice the students do. In encounters with stable, monogamous families, a clinician would likely choose a static model. However, if the family is dispersed among several households, or composed of serial relationships, the clinician might discover that genograms are not enough.

Genograms Are Not Enough: Family Imaging in a Historic Perspective

The history of graphic imaging of families may be the beginning of network thinking in social sciences. The affinograph is a method to advance that thinking along the lines proposed by Alvin Wolfe:

> The network analyst does not conceive a social network that is structurally fixed, does not reify the patterns of relations observed, does not attribute purpose to them. Purpose enters only at the level of the elementary relation, which has persons transacting. Yet, the network approach does not entail reductionism, for the relation itself is more than the sum of its parts. Network theory, when it develops, will generalize about relations among relations, how transactions affect such relations, how such relations affect transactions (Wolfe 1978, p. 56).

In spite of its promising beginning, the network thinking has not penetrated the applied fields of family sciences. Person-centered graphic representations, such as pedigrees and genograms, still dominate even as static models become less applicable. It seems that the family imaging methods are still closer to the original family trees than to "generalizations about relations among relations" (Wolfe 1978, p. 56).

The most enduring representational method, the family tree, has been in use at least since the ninth century (Freeman 2004, p. 21). A family tree visually connects the names of one generation to the next revealing the lineage of the mother on the one side and the father on the other side of the family tree. Nothing changed in the use of family trees until a thousand years later anthropologists Morgan (1870/1997) and Macfarlane (1883) introduced circles and lines to represent relationships within and across generations among various cultures around the world.

Another method of family imaging developed independently from anthropology. Nineteenth-century eugenicists standardized a set of symbols used to construct *pedigrees.* Pedigree symbols have been retained in the modern day genograms. Davenport (1911/1972), Goddard (1912), and Wiggam (1924) published works using pedigree images of families that identify males with squares and females with circles. They arranged circles and squares in stacked horizontal rows. As in a genogram, each horizontal row represented a generation. Another pedigree remnant found in genograms was the use of vertical lines to join parents with their children.

Early in the twentieth century, a British anthropologist W. H. R. Rivers expanded the applications of the family tree and pedigrees to represent marriage customs, boundaries of totemism, and demographic characteristics of marriage partners (Rivers 1900, 1910). These early conventions of associating individual traits with the graphic symbols are similar to the way genograms are used in family assessment today (Becvar and Becvar 2000, pp. 155–180; Bowen 1978; Goldenberg and Goldenberg 2008, p. 193; McGoldrick and Gerson 1985; McGoldrick et al. 2008; Titelman 2003). A part of that historical convention is a method of representing generations by relative positioning of symbols.

The rigid positioning of symbols precludes applications of the network or graph theory in general. Consequently, the use of genograms becomes limited to more stable family systems. Minor variations in the use of geometric symbols could not compensate for the drastic changes that the family has undergone in America over the twentieth century. In psychiatry, genetics, social work, and family therapy, a square has represented a male and circle a female since the inception of these professions. Horizontal lines connecting a square and a circle indicate a marriage. Anthropologists and sociologists varied their representational techniques slightly. Instead of a square to represent a male, they used a triangle. The circle stood for a female across all disciplines. Instead of a line connecting a triangle and a circle, an equal sign has been used. Sociologists reserved the square to represent "other gender," "gender unknown," or "gender unspecified" (Winch and Goodman 1968, p. 142). Instructional manuals on genograms do not acknowledge that sometimes two genders are not enough (Devor 2009).

Imaging Changes in Family Systems

Changes in family systems demand changes in methods of family imaging. The change in family structure is accompanied with a change in the meaning of relationships. Historically, being married meant being removed from the field of eligibles for mate selection. The term *field of eligibles* referred to single people of legal age and opposite gender. It was taken for granted that marriage was between a man and a woman who were expected to live together until one died. Most remarriages occurred after death of a spouse, a condition easily represented by a genogram. These stable families centered on biological parents and their children. Step parenting after divorce and parenting without marriage were rare. It was assumed that each child had exactly one father and one mother.

An argument in favor of affinographs is that "it is no longer the case that a child born today can expect to live his or her childhood with both biological parents" (Teachman et al. 2000, p. 1243). As marriage bonds weakened, married people continued to be available whether or not they had children (Cherlin 2004; Farber 1964). By the 1990s, the traditional mate selection, marriage, and childbearing became a special case (Cherlin 2005; Kephart and Jedlicka 1991; Kreider and Fields 2002; Kreider 2005). Because of these changes, it has become more difficult to define the human family. Without a definition, however, we cannot understand that what we study. Therein lies another reason for "why affinographs": An affinograph can serve as a model between a general definition of the human family and the specific real-world manifestations of family systems.

Affinographs and a Definition of the Human Family

I am seeking a definition of the human family that is discernible as a graphic image in any culture, in any historical period, and without a predilection toward any family form or gender combination. Ideally, the definition should include both structural and functional rudiments of a family system at a high level of generality. Even though there is a long history of grappling with the definitions of the human family, the literature remains pessimistic even about the possibility of such a definition. A long-standing view among family scientists has been that there are only situational definitions. Robert Winch, one of the most prominent family sociologists of the twentieth century, commented in 1952 that the scientific definition of the family is a matter of sheer expediency:

> In scientific writing, however, there has arisen the convention of the author's privilege to define as he pleases, so long as his definition is explicit and his use of it consistent. Let us conclude, therefore, that the criteria of a "good" scientific definition are not those of "truth" and "rightness," but rather the utility of the term, or what it enables us to see when we set about to use it (Winch 1952, p. 13).

Winch concluded that the most suitable definition is "one which is most consistent with the task at hand" (Winch 1952, p. 14). Almost fifty years later, in a seminal book entitled *Concepts and Definitions of Family for the 21st Century* (Settles et al. 1999), Holstein and Gubrium reiterate Winch's view under the rubric of *social constructionism:* "Our view, as far as family is concerned, is that there is no 'given' relationship between reality and representation. Rather, the relationship is eminently social and contingent, one of our own making" (Holstein and Gubrium 1999, p. 17).

Over 50 years since Robert Winch wrote about the definition of the family, his assumptions remained a hallmark for family sciences: If something is subjective, situational, or culture-bound, then there is no higher level of abstraction that could define commonality of function and structure across cultures and disciplines. Possibly, because of such thinking, there has been little progress toward developing a consensus on the universal meaning of the human family. Settles (1999) sums it best: "If there ever was a consensus on the definition of the family, it is not to be found in today's research and policy analysis" (p. 209). Nor, according to some experts, are we likely to reach consensus soon (Segrin and Flora 2005, p. 4).

Po Bronson, an American journalist and a critic, gives some reasons why social scientists have failed to reach a consensus on the meaning of the word *family:*

> In my book, I spend a lot of time critiquing those who want to define or label a family, so it may seem ironic to have a page of nothing but definitions of "family." But I think that these actually show the fruitlessness of the exercise. Because in that single word are social, historical and cultural values. Embedded in how it's defined are decrees about what's a social norm. Or acceptable behavior. It tells people who's in and who's out. What counts as a family and what doesn't. It's obvious just by reading some of these, some have really been politicizing the family, while others have tried to go with the most pragmatic of definitions. None of these will give you a sense of reassurance. You can't use them to say, "So, we're a family!" (Bronson 2005)

Failing to define the human family so that the definition indeed corresponds to reality may have dire consequences. Dinerman (2004) describes how government agencies define families to suit the political climate of the day. It is reasonable to conjecture, for example, that in the absence of an authoritative, scientific definition, the family status in the society weakens in relation with other social institutions. When experts on the human family cannot agree on the rudimentary structure and function of a family, then other institutions are more likely to use the family as a resource for their own maintenance. Some anecdotal evidence comes from my own field observations. I know of a dying man who threatened to shoot at social workers, because they would not accept his definition of his own family. I have talked to a young man who had to hide from the officials so that the mother of his children could get health care and food stamps. The agency providing services for his children defined him out of the family. These anecdotes support the hypothesis that in the absence of an authoritative agreement among social scientists on what constitutes a family, any definition will stand unchallenged no matter how damaging it may be to individuals and their families.

Experts might find some grounds for agreement if they focus on the universal concepts in family sciences. A consensus could be reached if we adopt what Wolfe (1978) termed *network thinking.* Ordinary people already think in terms of networks, and they have no problems defining their own families. I recently attended a family reunion in which 29 people posed for their "family" picture. When they looked at the picture each one could say with complete reassurance "We're a family." When asked, "Was everyone there?" they knew exactly who was missing and why. If I prepared an affinograph of everyone in that picture and then added those who were absent, there would be a consensus of the feeling "That is our family!"

Now imagine a project where you have the resources to select randomly any residence in the world. Ask a person at that residence to organize a "family reunion." Even if the culture you selected does not have a concept of a family reunion, you could certainly explain it to them and begin planning. Let us say you had a year to complete the project. It is almost certain that anywhere in the world you could get a group of people together as a family. If all the kin lived close together, a reunion might be easy to assemble. In another location, the family may be gathered from different parts of the world. In fact, people in every culture know whom to invite, how to contact them, and how to relate to them. Their behaviors would reveal network thinking in everyday life. If network thinking is a universal reality in everyday life, then a universal definition of the family should follow from these observed network concepts.

Even though the experts have failed to agree on what constitutes a family, the effort to reach a consensus is far from futile. When the onus for providing a definition is placed on the ego instead of an "expert," the clarity emerges. The definition of the family proposed below corresponds to the affinograph assumptions. Because a family's composition can change over a person's life span, such a definition should include family relations, past and present, from birth to death. Even though the following definition lacks mathematical formality, it is robust and inclusive:

> A family is a changing network of three or more relationships accumulated through descent and affinal unions such as marriage, civil unions, or informal unions, with an opportunity or an expectation to procreate, adopt, and raise children.

Let us examine this definition, phrase by phrase, starting with *changing network*. This phrase implies that relationships are dynamic: People die; children are born; ritual kin are added to the family; divorces and remarriage have become an acceptable pattern. The change goes on from generation to generation and within generations. In American society, the change in networks includes serial sexual partners and the possibility of parenting in multiple relationships. The phrase "three or more relationships" emphasizes the "relationship among relationships." This phrase departs from the ego-centered perspective. It defines *a priori* two parents and a child as the smallest, naturally occurring building block of a family system. Whether biological parents are physically present or not, each person is assumed to be aware of his or her biological origin. The idea that a triad is the basic unit of a family system was proposed by Bowen (1978) and has been a justification for the use of genograms in family therapy (Guerin et al. 1996; Guerin and Pendagast 1976).

The phrase "accumulated through descent and affinal unions" is certainly a universally recognized component of family formation in every culture. There is no disagreement that families form through affinal unions. The disagreement comes from cultural differences in what constitutes an acceptable union. The "union" is a reality whether there is a disagreement or not. The phrase *an opportunity to procreate, adopt, and raise children* within those unions is also a "reality." Every culture provides opportunities with expectations to procreate or adopt children. Unions, procreation, or adoption occur in every culture; hence, it is possible to define a universally recognized family system.

The definition proposed above reflects network thinking and is a step toward understanding the universal meaning of the human family. The premise is that we cannot understand that which we cannot define whether or not we can image it. An image is not a definition. A mindless graphic image cannot be distinguished from a meaningful one without a general definition. The reductionist definitions such as the "single-parent family," definitions that equate a family with a household, or family definitions based on gender can all be imaged with affinographs or genograms. However, images unframed within a general definition neither elevate the discourse nor improve understanding.

A universal, nonreductionist definition may not initially fill the bill for all concerned. However, unless we make an effort to reach a consensus at least minimally, the ability of family professionals to influence social policy and improve the quality of family life is slim indeed. If the family professions are to function according to their ethics (Auger 1976; Bernstein and Hartsell 2000; Chase 2004; Denham 2003; Corey and Callanan 1993; Westermark 1994), it behooves them to consider "What is a Family?" without second-guessing those who already see themselves as a part of a family.

Affinograph Applications in Professions

New ideas are introduced into professions through education. Affinographs could introduce a universal definition of the family through courses in anthropology, family therapy, family medicine, psychology, sociology, social work, and other professions involved with families. Teaching, research, clinical practice, and services to families are collectively referred to here as "applications." Another answer to "Why affinographs?" is to promote interdisciplinary applications of family theory and method using the graph theory as an aid in network thinking.

Chapter 4 is intended to help social workers mediate between the demands of the state and the needs of families. Affinographs can help with tracking children and assessing the meaning of the family as defined by their clients.

Chapter 5 attempts to bridge the gap between licensed professional counselors and family therapists. Both groups of professionals encounter in their work the consequences of change in family structure. Counselors are encouraged to use affinographs when they suspect that complex relationships may influence the emotional state of the client. In such cases, affinographs can identify the relevant relationships and track them from session to session.

Affinographs are particularly suited for applications dealing with gay and lesbian family relationships. Family specialists who have used genograms with gay and lesbian couples (Feinberg and Bakeman 1994; Swainson and Tasker 2006; Weinstein 1992) may find affinographs more suitable for assessment of serial and ambiguous relationships. Affinographs can handle ambiguity by accepting varied meanings of the same relationship. The meaning of the same relationship can vary with the points of views of the parents, children, and the same-gender partner. Chapter 6 will focus specifically on affinographs applications pertaining to family formation and dissolution among gay and lesbian couples. Chapter 7 introduces ephemeral and extadyadic relations as they influence the quality and duration of primary relations among either the same-gender or different-gender couples.

The potential for application of network ideas in family therapy is explored in Chap. 8. This chapter builds on the *network paradigm* introduced into the practice of family therapy by Pattison (1981). Chapter 8 addresses the question posed by Pattison: "How do we effectively discriminate between the use of social network paradigms as a method of clinical evaluation, as a method for organizing different clinical treatment programs, and as a specific clinical treatment intervention per se?" (Pattison 1981, p. 244). The network paradigm, Pattison and others have employed since then, has been restricted to the *person networks* (Gameiro et al. 2010; Hansen et al. 1991; Hurd et al. 1981; Keams and Leonard 2004; Rao et al. 2001; Sluzki 2010).

Traditionally, family imaging in genealogical trees has also been person based. Because affinographs images focus on relationships, let us call this application *affinology*. Chapter 9 demonstrates the utility of this method by imaging descent of some of the most complicated families in America, including the family of President Obama.

To apply affinographs for any of the purposes listed above some skills are required. The following chapter will describe how to construct affinographs for use in education, research, clinical interventions, and even genealogy.

Chapter 3
How to Construct Affinographs

Abstract This chapter provides the basic symbols to image present and past ephemeral and committed relationships. Open and closed adoptions are distinguished and presented as a special case of descent. A method for mapping households independently from affinal relationships is described for possible use in social work. The key symbols are circles and lines. Circles represent past and present relationships and lines between circles represent descent or change of partners. Algebraic notations are used to track children as their parents change partners and households.

Affinographs can be constructed using pencil and paper or with computer programs. The most convenient method is a pencil and paper. Hand drawings during clinical sessions serve as a shortcut for notetaking while providing visual images of the client's family. Another way to draw an affinograph is with the *shapes* options in the Microsoft Office programs. Shapes function in the Microsoft Word can be used for insertion of graphs into written documents and in the Microsoft Power Point for use in teaching. The Microsoft Office Visio 2007 (Holzner 2008) is a program designed specifically for graphic applications. The guiding principle of Visio is that "a picture is worth a thousand words." That principle transfers to affinographs whether drawn by hand, "Shapes," or with Visio.

Regardless of the level of technology used, affinograph symbols and rules are identical. The affinograph uses circles to identify past and present relationships, lines to identify descent and serial relationships, and algebraic symbols to track children as their parents change partners and households. Shortcut symbols can be used to identify the type of affinal union and to associate traits with people. The use of shortcut symbols is optional and is kept to the minimum. Parsimony is valued.

To master the basic applications of affinographs, a user needs to learn symbols to represent past and present relationships and changes in relationships. A method is also proposed for identifying households.

D. Jedlicka, *Affinographs*, DOI 10.1007/978-1-4419-9395-3_3,

Representing Past and Present Relationships

An affinograph differentiates between ongoing relationships, also referred to as *present* relationships, and terminated relationships or *past* relationships. A present relationship is represented with a solid circle:

A circle can stand for any type of relation: marital, nonmarital, same-gender, ephemeral, cohabiting, polygamous, or whatever an observer encounters in interaction with the observed. Each relation can be identified by type and in relation to other generations. There could be different conventions of labeling a relationship. One convention uses words. As an example, let us say that the observer wants to identify all the members represented with a solid circle:

John (38) & Magdalene (40), married (2000)
Children: Mark (5), Pat (8), Sam (9)

Another way to label relies on abbreviations: M (2000), 2s (5,9), d(8). "M" is for marriage followed by the year of marriage. Throughout this book "d" will stand for daughter and "s" for son. In cases where the child's gender is not known a letter "c" will stand for child. Two "d" means that there are two daughters with the numbers in the parenthesis indicating their age at the time of observation. The year of birth could be included instead.

A past relationship is represented with an empty circle. An empty circle indicates that the relationship ended before death of either partner. Let us say that John and Magdalene divorced.

Their story could be summed with a circle and a caption (b is for "born"):

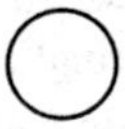

John (b1971) & Magdalene (b1969), M.2000, div.2010
(2s(2005, 2002), d(2001)) left with mother.

An empty circle with one or two slashes indicates relationship terminated through death:

died2009   

Death of a Male | Death of a Female | Death of Both

The slash representing death of a male slants to the right for a reason. The symbol for a male historically has been a circle with an arrow pointing up to the right. This ancient convention should make it easy to remember: A slash to the right stands for death of a male, and a slash in the opposite direction for death of a female. When both parents or partners die two slashes are combined. The abbreviation for "death" is "dd" followed by the year of death.

In cases of deaths involving the same-gender partners or adoptive parents, two slashes clearly convey the meaning (dd stands for "died"):

For the sake of completeness, and to acknowledge that two genders may not always be enough to classify self-reported identity of partners, a symbol for death of a person of unknown or "other" gender is a vertical line through an empty circle:

There is one more logical possibility that can be represented with a circle: In cases where the observer cannot discern whether a relationship is current or terminated, a filled or an empty circle would be misleading. To account for the unknown status of a relationship, we can use either an empty or a filled circle with a question mark in it "?":

Circles themselves are not very interesting unless they become a part of a network of accumulated relationships of descent and affinity. To represent relations among relations over time requires the use of lines in conjunction with circles.

Representing Change Among Relationships

Ever since the nineteenth century, it has been customary to divide family relationships into *consanguine* and *affinal*. In affinographs, the word *consanguine* was omitted without loss of clarity. Instead, the affinograph definition, and the general definition of the human family that followed from it, use the term *descent,* which includes intergenerational ties without regard to consanguinity. Adoptions are equated to procreation using the term *descent*. Children are considered descendents of their parents no matter how they entered the family.

A descent line in an affinograph indicates a formation of a relationship within which procreation or adoption of children is a reasonable expectation. If a person never procreates or adopts, the affinograph associates that person with the family of origin only. In other words, the descent line stops if no child in the family establishes an affinal relationship. The descent line indicates the gender of the person forming a relationship. Different types of lines represent males, females, and other or unknown gender as follows:

A solid line represents a male.
A dotted line is used to represent a female, and
a "Morse Code" line represents an "unknown" or "other" gender.

A line connects two points, actually two circles. It is essential to know which circle represents the family of origin and which circle represents a new affinal relationship. One way to know is to write on the graph "family of origin" or FO. However, most affinographs represent images of several relationships and several generations. Writing descriptive labels for each relationship would become unmanageable. To add information without losing parsimony, a subscript is assigned to algebraic symbols attached to each filled or empty circle.

The value of the subscript reveals the sequence of two relations. To illustrate this method, let us use John and Magdalene's case from above. Assuming that their parents are alive and married to each other, subscripts associated with each marriage, M, distinguishes the family of origin from the family of descent.

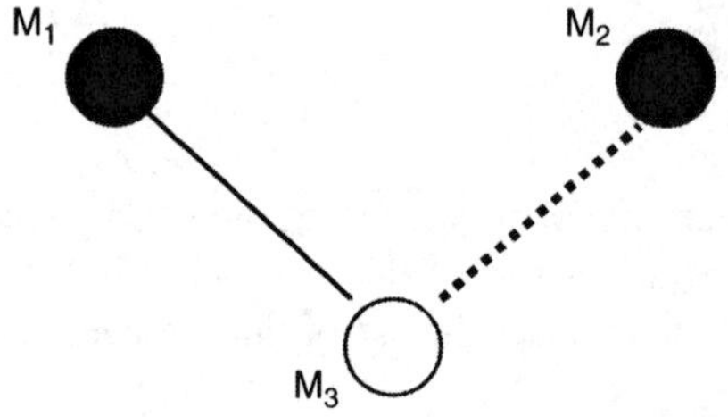

John (1971) & Magdalene (1969), M.2000, div, 2010
(2s(2005, 2002), d(2001)) left with mother.

The rule is that the highest value subscript in the preceding generation is lower than the lowest value subscript in the current generation. This numbering system may start either with the oldest generations or the youngest generations first. In the case of John and Magdalene, the oldest generation is numbered first: M_1 represents

John's parents and M_2 Magdalene's parents. The system would also work in reverse. For example, in the case of the affinology of President Obama in Chap. 9, subscript "one" is applied to the president's immediate family with subscript values increasing with each preceding generation. Either way, any two subscripts connected with a line will immediately reveal which relationship came first.

Just as three types of nondirected lines are enough to image descent, three types of directed lines are also enough to image serial relationships. A directed line emanates from a terminated relationship and ends in a subsequent relationship. Directed lines, the same as nondirected lines, can take on one of three shapes: solid, dotted, or "Morse Code."

A solid directed line represents a male leaving one relationship and forming another relationship.

A dotted directed line represents a female leaving one relationship and forming another relationship.

A "Morse Code" line represents the unknown or "other" genders.

At this point, there are enough symbols to construct affinographs in actual clinical settings. A case in my experience as an intern in a brain injury clinic can serve to illustrate how affinograph symbols can be used to represent dramatic changes in a person's family. The clinic was responsible for housing severely brain-injured patients until they could find a place for permanent care. More than half of about sixty cases that went through the clinic in about six months involved some issue with the parents or intimate partners. In one such case the father became sexually involved with his son's fiancé.

The affinograph in Fig. 3.1 illustrates this case. Charles, a man in his mid-twenties, from a household with two married parents M_1, became engaged to marry a woman whose parents were also married, M_2. The engagement, represented as a nonmarital relationship N_3, terminated when Charles discovered that his fiancé was in love with his father. The father actually filed for a divorce with the intent to marry his son's fiancé. The son in a fit of anger drove his car at speeds over 100 miles per hour and hit an embankment. The police report recorded the event as an "accident." After that "accident" Charles spent three months on life support system and emerged bound to a wheelchair with irreversible brain damage. The father divorced his mother and moved out to an unknown location with his son's former fiancé. The letter "R" indicates that the type of the relationship was not known. A question mark within the circle indicates that it was also not known whether the relationship terminated or not.

In general, letter "R" can stand for any affinal relationship. The relation R can be unknown, undefined, ambiguously defined, or variously defined. On a less abstract level, relation R could take on a specific meaning as provided by the observed, the ego. The most common affinal relations are marital, cohabitation, relations dealing

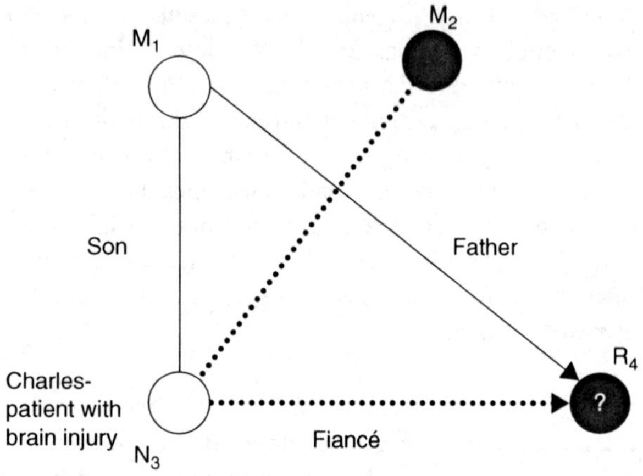

Fig. 3.1 Father divorces and elopes with his son's fiancé

with adoption, ephemeral relations with an opportunity to procreate (John Edwards, Democratic Party's candidate for president in 2008, comes to mind), and polygamous marriages would probably exhaust most of the possibilities anywhere in the world. If not, an observer can always add new symbols as needed. Some suggested relationship symbols include:

R =

- M = marriage, monogamous or polygamous
- N = nonspecific, nonmarital relationship
- C = cohabitation
- A = biological parents of an adopted child
- E = ephemeral sexual relationships without expectation of attachment
- O = lasting affairs. ("O" is for "other" than the primary partner).

Note that there is no "same-gender" marriage relationship designation. That is a strength of the affinograph method of imaging. An affinograph implies no judgment about what gender combinations make up a marriage and a family. Same-gender relations are labeled, defined, and assessed using the same criteria as the different-gender relations.

Labels for relations are not sufficient to incorporate infants and dependent children into today's complicated family networks. To make an affinograph more useful for tracking children requires the use of subscripts. How to use these notations to track children as they change households from birth to the current residence is described next.

Using Affinographs to Track Children

Inability to track children is a recurring problem in agencies providing services to families. When parents stay together for life and restrict all childbearing to a monogamous relationship, it is easy to track their children and provide temporary services. However, when parents procreate with a series of partners, tracking children and identifying parents can be problematic. Affinographs can improve methods of tracking children even in networks involving multiple households. It is only necessary to apply the simplest algebraic notations to allow for accurate and complete tracking of children in time and space.

In an affinograph, children are tracked from birth to the current household. With time, parents can change partners, and children may follow one parent or another. Through changes in relationships of parents, biological parents may be replaced with *significant others*, or significant others can be added as additional objects of attachment. The phrase "significant other" is used here as originally proposed by Mead (1934) and taught in sociology for decades (Broom and Selznick 1968, p. 97). A significant other is any family member responsible for socialization and care of a child.

Because each relationship in an affinograph is assigned a unique number, it is possible to identify children's associations with significant others from birth to the most recent residence. A unique identification number does not have to be a subscript. The number can be placed anywhere as long as it is clearly associated with a specific relationship. However, it is conventional to identify the series with subscripts; hence, I will use subscripts throughout this book.

To illustrate tracking with subscripts, I use the letter "*d*" to stand for "*daughter*," and the letter "*s*" to stand for "*son*." A child's name can also be used in conjunction with subscripts. Preceding the list of children is a capital letter identifying the marital status of the significant others within the household in which the child resides. A subscript is associated with each child as follows: If a child was born in another relationship then the subscript associated with the child is equal to the subscript of the relationship at birth. In general, children in their current household can be identified as follows:

$$R_j \; s_n, \; d_n$$

When *n* equals *j*, means the child was born in the current relationship. In that case, it may be expedient not to use subscripts. Simply, R, s, d implies that the children were born to parents in the current relationship. If a parent lived with a child in more than two relationships, subscripts can be added to indicate each previous relationship involving that child. For example, let us say that a child, *c*, was born to a married couple M_1. Then, the couple divorced and the mother formed a new marriage, M_2. After a few years, that marriage terminated. The mother married for the third time, M_3, bringing her child with her. Subscripts attached to letter "*c*", $c_{1,2,3}$ indicate that the child was born in M_1, lived in M_2 until that marriage ended, and is now living with the stepfather in M_3.

Fig. 3.2 John and Magdalene's children and family

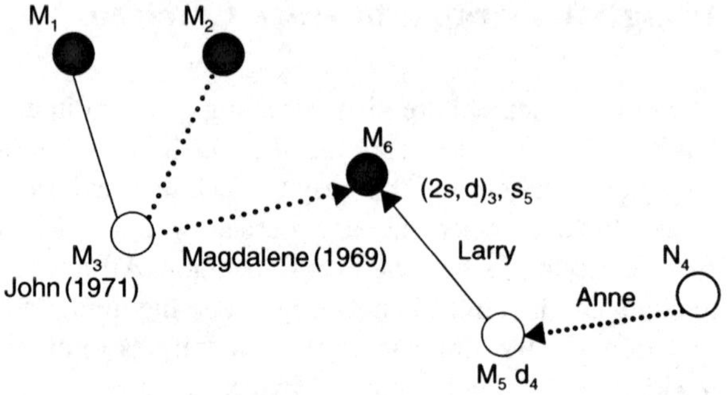

We can add more information about children. In addition to recording the gender of each child, one can also record the names and ages or years of birth:

R_j s(Mark, 2005)$_n$, d(Pat, 2002)$_n$, s(Sam, 2001)$_n$

To see how this looks in an affinograph, follow John's and Magdalene's children through an affinograph in Fig. 3.2. Note that after the divorce, the children were left with their mother. She remarried, M_6, a divorced man, Larry, who had one child from a previous marriage, M_5. The notation s_5 indicates that Larry's child was born in relationship M_5. The daughter d_4 in relationship M_5 shows that Larry's previous wife, Anne, had a child with another man in relationship N_4. Subscript "3" associated with each of Magdalene's children shows that all were born in a previous marriage, M_3.

A special case of tracking children in relation to their birth parents and nonbiological significant others is adoption. Below is a method for tracking children who may be adopted through open adoption or closed adoption.

Tracking Adopted Children

Adoptions can be open or closed. An open adoption allows contact between biological and adoptive parents. The adopted child in an open adoption generally knows the biological parents and may even have some contact with them. In a closed adoption, confidentiality is important, and the identity of the adoptive parents may not be known to the biological parents.

These two types of adoption have different representations in an affinograph. In each case, the biological parents' relationship, whatever it may be, is labeled with a capital letter "*A*". The letter "*A*" in some cases of open adoption may be coupled with the relationship label if known as in the case shown in Fig. 3.3. An isolated circle with a question mark can be used to represent a closed adoption:

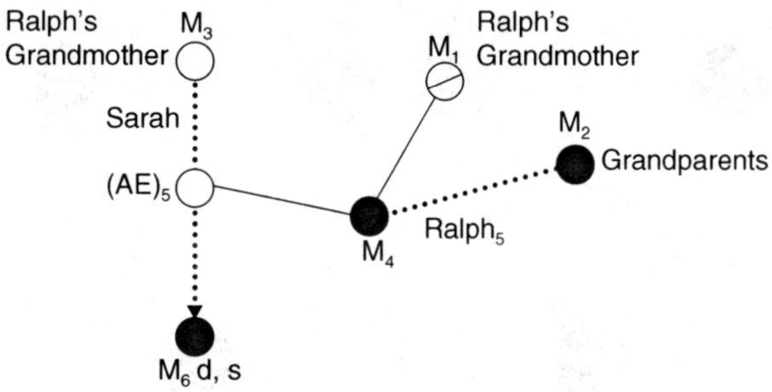

Fig. 3.3 A case of an open adoption

In this example, the married couple, M_2, has adopted a daughter from unknown parents A_1. The same married couple has their own biological son, s_2.

Figure 3.3 shows an open adoption. The adopted child in Fig. 3.3 was born to a teenage mother, Sarah, shown in affinograph as $(AE)_5$. "*E*" stands for an ephemeral relationship. As a result of a casual encounter during the last year in high school, Sarah became pregnant without intending to marry son Ralph's father. Sarah's parents were divorced, M_3 and unable to help her raise her son. The solid line, linking Sarah with the married couple, M_4, shows an open adoption. Sarah married later and had two children in that marriage, M_6,(*d, s*). Ralph's family consists of his adaptive parents, his mother Sarah, her current husband, his half sister, and half brother and his grandparents. What is interesting about Ralph's case are the relationships with his grandparents. Ralph was in touch with Sarah's mother, M_3 his adoptive father's mother M_1 and adoptive mother's parents M_2. His adoptive father's father was deceased and Sarah's father never established contact with Ralph.

The discussion on tracking children through social services continues in the next chapter. Social services generally associate their client with a single household. When the client moves without a notice, children may become lost to the system. In such instances, the lost children may be denied protection from neglect and abuse. A more efficient method of recording nonresidential households may reduce the number of children at risk.

Using Affinographs to Map Households

Measuring the degree of correspondence between households and families has been a challenge for decades (Ruggles and Brower 2003). Mapping households with the aid of an affinograph model may simplify the measurements. An affinograph requires a dedicated symbol that may not be confused with the labels used for family relationships. A logical dedicated symbol is the letter "*H*." A household as represented in an affinograph is a mutually exclusive concept from any relation "*R*." Let us give examples of four possibilities in identifying households *H*, and relations *R*.

Case I: One affinal relation and one household. This would be a typical nuclear family. Mother and father living together with children.

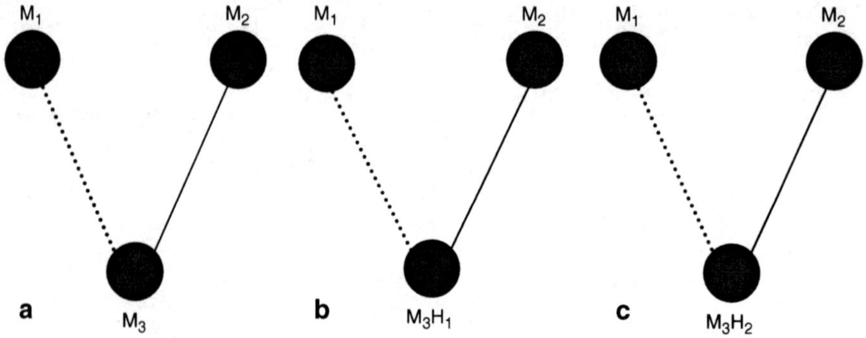

Fig. 3.4 A married couple living with parents. The subscript associated with the household "H" identifies the residence of a married couple

Case II: One household, multiple affinal relationships. An example would be an extended family with grandparents, parents, and children living under one roof.

Case III: One affinal relation and multiple households. Much research has been done with couples who cannot share a residence because they work at distant locations. Children may live with one or the other parent or in a third household with their grandparents.

Case IV: Multiple affinal relations, multiple households. Typically, living arrangements after divorce and remarriage fall into this category. Ironically, families officially identified as a single-parent family tend to be a segment of a larger network of households.

Case I needs no illustration. Two or more related people living within one residence are coterminous with a household and no additional labels are required. The case II may require some clarification of who is moving in with whom. Did the husband move in with his wife's parents or did the wife move in with her husband's parents? Generally, when two people marry and start their own household, there is no need for a special household designation. The case of a married couple stating their domicile separate from parents is illustrated in Fig. 3.4a. Figure 3.4b shows the husband moving in with the wife's parents, and Fig. 3.4c shows the wife moving in with the husband's parents. The subscript associated with the household "*H*" indicates who moved in with whom. When two subscripts match, the relationships and the household are coterminous.

The case of two different households for a husband and wife who remain married while maintaining separate residence can be identified by associating the household designation with the person rather than their relationship: John(H_1)/Marry(H_2).

Case IV involves networks of households and relationships in a variety of constellations. Chapters 4 through 8 will explore these constellations as they may be encountered in social work, counseling, and family therapy. A summary of symbols introduced above and used in the following chapters is included below.

Affinograph Symbol Guide

 Current relationship

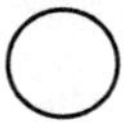 Past relationship

 Deceased male

 Deceased female

 Male and female partner deceased

 Two male partners deceased

 Two female partners deceased

 Deceased's gender unknown, undetermined or other

 Relationship status unknown

 Descent through a male

 Descent through a female

 Unknown or other gender

 A male leaving one relationship and forming another relationship

 A female leaving one relationship and forming another relationship

 A person of unknown or other gender leaving one relationship and forming another relationship

R =
- M = marriage, monogamous or polygamous
- N = nonspecific, nonmarital sexual relationship
- C = cohabitation
- A = biological parents of an adopted child
- E = ephemeral sexual relationships without expectation of attachment
- O = lasting affairs. ("O" is for "other" than primary partner)
- F = friendship

H = household
d = daughter
s = son
c = child
w = wife
h = husband
b = born
dd = died
m = married
div = divorced

Chapter 4
Critical Issues in Protecting Children and Serving Families

Abstract Research shows and experience confirms that families have changed and become more complex. Yet institutions and agencies offering social services to complex families have been slow in adapting to change. The affinograph method of initial assessment reveals that the notion of a "single-parent family" poorly corresponds with actual family constellations. The affinograph avoids preconceived notions of what the family ought to be and allows service providers to identify families from the client's perspective. Clearly defined families include nonresident parents and extended family. A systemic view of the family often clarifies sources of problems and leads to more lasting solutions. In general, affinographs help identify the need for integrated services across linked households and multiple generations.

Providing services for children and their parents in complex family networks can be a challenge. That challenge is exacerbated if the initial intake procedures omit relevant information, on the one hand, and overburden the case worker with volumes of individual-level information on the other. The existing techniques of questionnaire intakes tend to focus on resident parents and their children whether that focus is appropriate or not. According to the demographic trends, the proportion of families without both parents at one residence is increasing (Fields and Casper 2001), while the proportion of married people in the population is declining. The increase in officially designated single-parent families is associated with the increase in the demand for social services in housing, employment, income, health, and mental health (Fields 2003; Herzog et al. 2007; Maluccio et al. 2002; Sheafor et al. 2007).

The concept of a "single-parent family" commonly used for bureaucratic expedience tends to oversimplify the emerging complex families that social workers are likely to encounter (Parke 2004; Usdansky 2009). To define a family as a "*single-parent*" tends to isolate a parent from the family network distributed among several households. Failure to identify the interlocking households during the initial contact with a client is a reason social workers lose children entrusted to their oversight.

Failure to keep records of complex families can have serious consequences. Medical services and counseling can be terminated prematurely. Education, especially of home-schooled children, may be discontinued without the knowledge of state authorities responsible to enforce the compulsory education laws. Narrow def-

D. Jedlicka, *Affinographs*, DOI 10.1007/978-1-4419-9395-3_4,

initions of the family tend to exclude the kin who could help with care of children and the elderly. These limitations are discussed below as a background in support of the use of the affinograph method in the delivery of social services.

Limitations of Traditional Intake Assessment Procedures

The initial assessment of individuals and families tends to be a time-consuming ritual with questionable effectiveness even in child protection cases (Gibbons et al. 1995, p. 70; Trotter 2002). An intake procedure sometimes takes hours, yet the client's family boundaries remain a mystery to the case workers. Other partners and children residing elsewhere tend to be excluded even when they form a family from the client's point of view. Without noting who the relevant others are and where they live, the case worker limits the range of interventions and the ability to track mobile families.

The lack of the family system data is a common reason for agencies to lose children entrusted to their care. Because the official records focus on one person or one household, the agency is likely to lose track of the child when the family moves another location. Losing track of children is far more common than most people realize. Home-schooled children, abused children, and children who fail to attend school disappear from the system routinely. A parent may place the child with another member of the family or a friend (Moehling 2002). The data on missing children are available only if children are reported missing by their caretakers (Carmody 2000; Howard and Broughton 2004; Kappeler and Potter 2005). When the client no longer resides at the residence that appears in the official file, the case is closed.

The intake assessment proceeds according to the conceptual framework established by those who construct questionnaires and manage service agencies. A structured questionnaire represents the institutional version of reality often with minimum regard for the client. I reviewed dozens of intake questionnaires in use by social service agencies across the United States and found them to be poorly adapted to the family systems in America. For decades, it has been a common practice to focus on the individual in one household (Garrett 1982; Grbich 1999; Kadushin and Kadushin 1997; Kahn and Cannell 1957; Maple 1985; Pippin 1990; Sheafor et al. 2007). This inflexibility of the intake procedures could be at the root of what some researchers have identified as contradictions between policies and the reality of practice (Hudson et al. 1994; Parent et al. 2007).

A part of the failure to implement policies could also be related to the exclusion of nonresidential members of the child's family. Because mothers are a resident parent in most cases, fathers tend to be excluded from participation in the delivery of child and family services (Curran 2003; Dudley 2007; Horn 2006). This exclusionary practice continues even as mounting research shows that fathers also need help to be involved with their children (Anderson et al. 2002; Bunting and McAuley 2004; Fagan et al. 2007; Maza 2002a; Roggman et al. 2002). Both parents are important at every stage of the child's development (Fagan et al. 2007; Featherstone 2004; Hook 2006; McKinnon et al. 2001; Nelson 2005; Saleh et al. 2005; Summers et al. 2006).

The intake focus on a "single-parent family" limits the information about the family constellations and expands the information dealing with the focal person, usually a child. In the absence of a theoretically framed method for intake and assessment, there are thousands of different procedures used to assess the same problems. Each agency uses different intake and assessment forms with a plethora of questions, psychological batteries, behavioral inventories, and so on. Out of thousands of these instruments and evaluation procedures, it appears that few are reliable and valid.

In short, the current intake procedures tend to omit the relevant family relations and overemphasize the individual information that is rarely used. Because it is widely recognized that families have become more complex and diverse (Carstens 2001; Earls and Carlson 2001; Manning et al. 2007; Parent et al. 2007; Reitman et al. 1995; Roser-Strier 2001), "practitioners should always inquire about the composition of the family" (Steiner 2004, p. 54). Traditional techniques of inquiry have not kept pace with the assessment needs of varied and complex families found in America today. The section below offers a method of assessment that includes a wider range of family types.

The Affinograph Method of Family Assessment

The affinograph method empowers the client to define one's own significant relationships. This method identifies systemic problems and leads to systemic solutions as suggested in the related literature (Cooley 2000; Gee and Rhodes 2003; Kenney 2004; Kielty 2005; Kohler et al. 2004). In general, the affinographs are constructed from notes taken during a face-to-face interview. If more than one family member is present, each member is interviewed, including every child old enough to understand the questions.

Let us assume that the interviewee is the head of the household. The first question might be "Are your parents living?" The interviewer may pursue the constellation of the interviewee's parental household and each of the siblings in that household. When that segment of the family is identified, the questions then focus on children. Children may identify significant others who do not reside at the officially designated residence.

Research has shown that significant others help children behave better at home and in school (Coohey and Zhang 2006; Scourfield 2006; Wiemann et al. 2006). In my fieldwork, I encountered families receiving services under the designation of a "single-parent family" even though the focal child was attached to a nonresident member of the family. In some of these cases, the pull of the nonresident parent was a strong influence on the child, yet the official protocols would not authorize a social worker to place a phone call to a parent residing in another jurisdiction.

The interviewer pursues relevant relationships without a preordered set of questions. The goal is to record family ties according to the meaning they have to clients. Each person, including children, is free to define his or her own parentage regardless of biological ties. According to the affinograph assumptions, "each person has as many parents as that person identifies through experience." As a home visitation counselor, I encountered children whose mother's previous partner was the most significant person in child's life.

To ascertain the significance of each relationship, the interviewer asks: "Have you lived with anyone else before?" "Where is that person now?" "Is that person in a relationship with anyone else?" "Do you or your child have contact with the parents of…?" Such questions establish a family network that the interviewer jots on paper using symbols as explained in the chapter on "How to Construct Affinographs."

An affinograph may lead to the discovery of systemic problems even when the presenting problem is associated with a person. Cases below illustrate discrepancies between the presented problems and the actual problems. Each case below was at first presented as a behavioral problem involving a child. The assessment with the aid of an affinograph led to the identification of problems located elsewhere within the family network. These cases represent my observations as a family therapist for an agency providing intensive in-home therapy in a manner described by Barth et al. (2007).

The first case deals with a child whose mother was receiving public assistance under the designation of a "single-parent family." The second case shows the complexity of identifying nonresidential parents and siblings when they are crucial to the child's identity. The third case shows a three-generational family in need of integrated intergenerational services to solve the problems experienced by a child client.

Tracking Members of a "Single-Parent Family"

The term *single-parent family* in my experience with clients has been a myth. As soon as I begin to talk with children, the concept of a "single-parent family" becomes meaningless. To qualify for a state license to practice family therapy, I worked as a counselor with families whose children incurred some punitive action by the schools or the police. The overwhelming majority of these families were officially defined as "single-parent family headed by mother." This definition even excluded unmarried biological fathers who lived in the same household. Also excluded were the extended kin, biological parents living elsewhere, new partners of the live-in parent, and the current or past partners of the absent parent. Such exclusions made no exceptions for children who were attached to others in different jurisdictions. Several children had close relations with grandparents who lived else-

where. Parents' past and present partners also entered into the child's perceptions of the family network. Current partners whether perceived as unwelcome intruders or as objects of attachment loomed important in the lives of some children. Rather than being "a single-parent family," each family I encountered had emotional ties, negative or positive, with persons excluded from the official definition of the family.

Regardless of the official protocols, I would ascertain which relationships were important to whom. The results of my assessment would sometimes conflict with the institutional rules. The rules required that the child remains the client regardless of who actually contributed to the problem. The protocols of assessment and intervention required that one case equals one person, and that one person equals one residence. In the case that follows, the father was officially barred from participation in therapy.

Because families were more complex than officially recognized, I would prepare an affinograph to keep track of the actual family. The assessment using an affinograph most of the time changed the meaning of the official designation *identified client*. The term *identified client* seemed to isolate the client from the network of intricate emotional relations. Any reasonable therapist dealing with these cases could ascertain that the label was an oversimplification in the context of the family network identified by the client.

Figure 4.1 is an affinograph of one officially designated "single-parent family." This case opened when the mother reported to the police that her 17-year-old daughter, Joanna, assaulted her. Later, it turned out that this accusation was a gross exaggeration. Nevertheless, Joanna was placed on probation, and I was assigned to counsel her at her home. On my first visit, I found a twelve-year-old half-sister Patty, and a three-year-old half-brother, Sammy. Each of the three siblings in this household had the same mother and a different father. After the third week, the

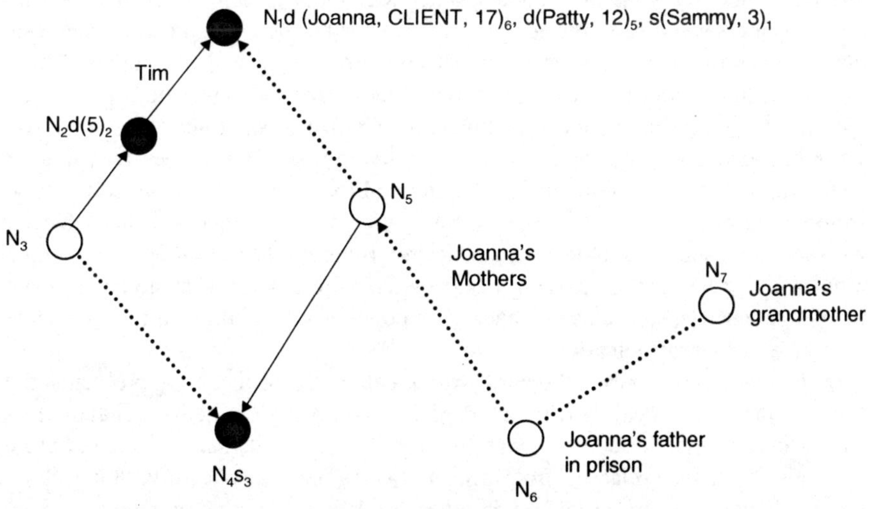

Fig. 4.1 A family constellation containing an officially designated "single-parent family," (N_1)

mother and Joanna trusted me enough to confide that Tim, Sammy's father, lived with them. Initially, they were afraid to reveal the father's presence out of fear of losing their state-provided benefits.

The affinograph in Fig. 4.1 shows that no one in this family was ever married. To understand what led to the conflict between mother and daughter, it was necessary to link the past with the present relationships.

Only the focal household, N_1 (d age $17)_6$, (d age $12)_5$, (s age $3)_1$ was identified in the official records. Tim, who shared children in two other households, N_2 and N_4, was never officially recognized as a member of this family. His youngest child, Sammy, was born in the current household. The filled circle indicates that this is the current relationship involving both parents within one household.

The relationship N_2 d$(5)_2$ shows that Tim is the father of a five-year-old daughter who lives with her mother at another residence. The circle, identifying the relationship N_2, remained full because Tim is also helping to raise his child in that relationship. In fact, that other relationship was an unresolved problem for Joanna. She considered Tim to be a bigamist and would tell him so. Tim would go back to live with his previous partner for several months before coming back to live several months with Joanna's mother. Joanna's mother, on the other hand, did not mind Tim's living arrangements. She felt that her relationship with Tim was not Joanna's concern. When Tim lived with one partner he would still visit the other regularly. Regardless of his residence, he helped with household chores and took care of the children when Joanna and her mother were unable to be at home. Joanna, unlike her mother, could not tolerate these living arrangements and would often argue about it with her mother and Tim.

Joanna, born in the relationship N_6, was her mother's first child This past relationship, more than Tim's living arrangements, was at the root of the family's consternation and a direct cause of Joanna's argument on the day her mother requested police intervention. Joanna's father was about to be released from prison after serving seven years of a longer sentence for murder. The literature suggests that incarceration can create extraordinary emotional upheaval for parents (Loper and Tuerk 2006) and children (Maza 2002b; Meek 2007). Joanna, who kept in touch with her father during his incarceration, was terrified of what her father might do when he came home and found another man living there. Her mother, on the other hand, did not want to talk about it. They argued for weeks. As her father's release from prison neared, Joanna panicked. She yelled at her mother and shook her by her shoulders, accidentally tearing the sleeve off her mother's blouse. Her enraged mother called the police charging her daughter with assault. Her mother showed the police her torn sleeve as evidence. The police handcuffed and arrested Joanna without a further investigation.

Even though my notes and records warned about the forthcoming problems, the scope of the agency dealing with this family was narrowly defined as behavioral issues strictly relating to Joanna. It was obvious that this family had to disperse before Joanna's father was released from prison. Joanna and Patty were thinking about moving in with their maternal grandmother, N_7. Joanna's mother was not sure what she would do. On my next visit, the house was empty, and Joanna was not at school. Because there were no provisions for follow-up, the case was closed.

Tracking Nonresidential Parents

It has been documented that public services often fail to help families whose values and living arrangements do not match institutional expectation (Cabrera and Peters 2000; Marsiglo and Day 2000; Moss 2003; Peterson and Steinmetz 2000; Strug and Wilmore-Schaeffer 2003; Summers et al. 2004, 2006). Family constellations formed through a series of casual unions may not conform to academic definitions or bureaucratic protocols. The affinograph, on the other hand, visually represents the structure, boundaries, and functions of such families as perceived by those involved in them.

The affinograph shown in Fig. 4.2 represents the relationship history as reported by a twenty-four-year-old, Susanne, and her eight-year-old son Billy. Billy was an identified client, because he caused disruptions in school. Billy was Susanne's first child. From age sixteen through twenty-four Susanne gave birth to four children, each with a different father. It was important for Billy to feel secure within this family. Billy doubted his mother's ability to stay in a relationship and was apprehensive about what each day would bring. Looking at the affinograph in Fig. 4.2, it appeared that Billy's fears were justified.

The first relevant affinograph point in Fig. 4.2 stands for the relationship E_1. At the time that relation occurred, Susanne was a sixteen-year-old and sexually active with her classmate Steve. That ephemeral relation resulted in pregnancy and birth

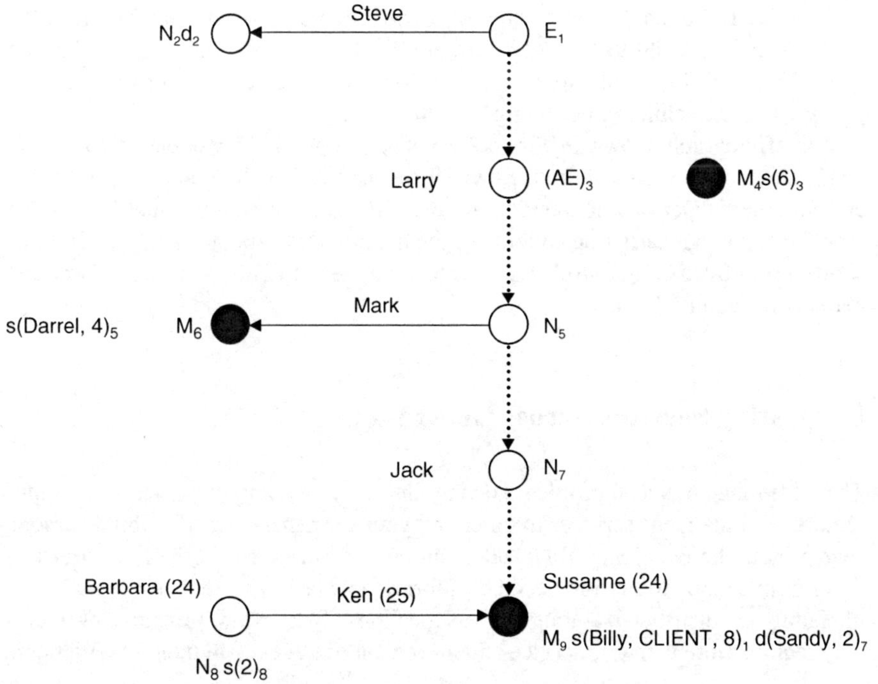

Fig. 4.2 Tracking nonresident parents

of Susanne's first child, Billy. At the same time, Susanne was involved with drugs and the police. Steve was never asked to be accountable as Billy's father. Within a year of Billy's birth, Steve cohabited, N_2 and had a second child, Billy's half sister. Steve did not financially support either of his children.

The relationship designated as $(AE)_3$ shows that Susanne became pregnant again through casual sex. Because she had more than one casual partner, her best guess was that Larry was the father. Without being sure who the father was, and having the responsibility for her first child, Susanne requested the services of an adoption agency. The symbol "*A*" identifies the family of birth of the adopted child. The letter M_4 shows a married couple who adopted Susanne's son. Number six after the letter "*s*" shows that the adopted son was six years old at the time of the interview. The isolated circle associated with this marriage represents a closed adoption.

After Susanne had given her son for adoption, she cohabited with Mark, N_5. They lived together until the birth of her third child, Darrel. Susanne did not seem to be able to cope with two children and a partner. She reverted to taking drugs and seeing other men. Because Mark could not accept such a relationship, he left with his child. Mark moved in with another woman whom he later married, M_6. Susanne has not been in touch with Mark. Billy, however, is aware that he has two half brothers elsewhere.

In less than six months after Mark left her, Susanne moved in with Jack, N_7. At age 22, she gave birth to her fourth child, Sandy. Susanne had two children to raise with a partner who did not want the responsibility for raising them. Susanne left Jack and became friends with Ken. Susanne and Ken married, M_9, after he terminated his cohabiting relationship with Barbara, N_8. Susanne was not a cause of that breakup, even though they met while Ken was still residing with Barbara. Ken left his two-year-old child to live with Barbara. He kept regular visitations of his son and helped with financial support. Unlike Ken, Susanne severed her ties with her past partners and children not living with her.

The affinograph shown in Fig. 4.2 reveals a network of resident and nonresident parents with their children. Steve, for example, is Billy's nonresident father and Susanne is Darrel's nonresident mother, M_6. Billy was afraid that his mother would resort to her earlier behaviors. As she thought more about her future, Susanne showed improved self-control. As she changed, her son Billy became calmer and better behaved in school.

Integrating Services Across Generations

The wide range of social problems facing families in a complex society sometimes requires simultaneous services to older and younger generations distributed among several households (Cohn et al. 2004; Simon and Burns 1997). Keeping track of cases from session to session becomes a formidable task when households of a single family are distributed among various localities. To help families solve problems may require more than one service and more than one agency to interact with them.

Affinographs can help track and coordinate services in such complex cases. A case from my clinical experience illustrates the usefulness of an affinograph for tracking progress from session to session. The case initially involved a thirteen-year-old girl, Nancy, who lived with her mother Bonnie and six-year-old sister Paula. Nancy, an "A" student, suddenly started getting poor grades, used inappropriate language to teachers, and started fights in school. Also, her sister Paula cried more than usual for a child.

The initial assessment ascertained that each girl had a different father. Both fathers were in contact with Bonnie even though neither resided with her. As is usually the case, nonresident fathers had limited economic resources (Cancian and Meyer 2004), but remained motivated to stay in contact with their welfare-attached children. The girls' grandmother also loomed significant, because the girls could escape from the household conflict by spending time with their grandmother in a nearby neighborhood.

Figure 4.3 shows three generations. The middle generation includes Bonnie and two fathers. The fathers are identified in the affinograph as Bonnie's "boyfriend 1" and "boyfriend 2." Each boyfriend lives at a separate residence, indicated on the affinograph as household H_x and H_y. Boyfriend 1 is Nancy's father and boyfriend 2 is Paula's father. Bonnie continued to interact with both boyfriends when they came to visit their daughters. Occasionally, these two men would visit Bonnie at the same time. Each boyfriend perceived the other as a rival. Arguments often ensued, sometimes requiring police intervention. In anticipation of conflict or for privacy,

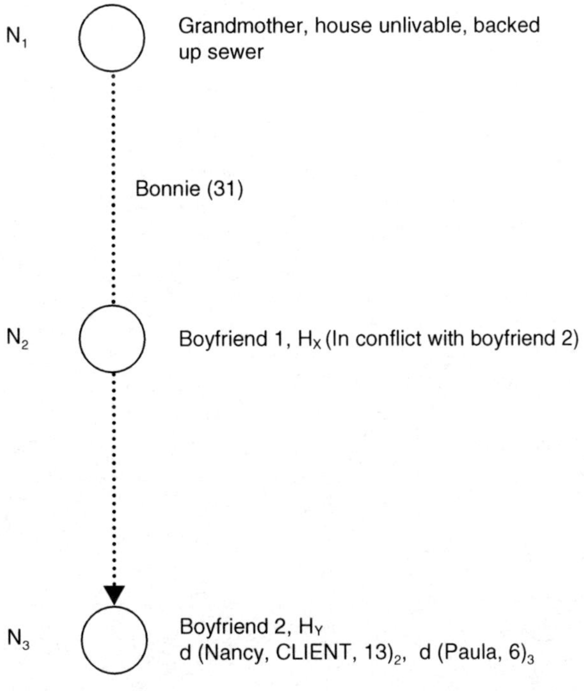

Fig. 4.3 A three-generation family in need of integrated services

Nancy and Paula would go to their grandmother's house where they could study and play in a calm environment.

One day the septic tank at the grandmother's house backed up. None of the family members had enough money to hire a plumber. The house was unlivable. Nancy became agitated and easily prone to anger when she could no longer escape there. The girls described the odors as unbearable. The case that began with a thirteen-year-old girl as a focal client led to external issues that helped explain her reactivity.

Helping the grandmother regain her home was obviously the key issue in this case. Bonnie's home could hardly hold the furniture and have enough space to walk. Grandmother was overweight and literally too large to live with Bonnie. As difficult as it was for this family to live in a small space, a greater problem was that the girls lost their refuge from conflict. It took four weeks for me and a social worker to find some help for the grandmother. Finally, a church group offered to help and restore the house. Once grandmother's home became livable again, the girls calmed down. They could again retreat to the grandmother's house and avoid confrontations between their mother and their fathers.

There were other segments of this family not shown in Fig. 4.3. Each boyfriend also had living mothers and fathers, brothers and sisters. However, none of them had any contact with the girls, and they were unwilling to help with the work needed to make the grandmother's house livable again. While counseling helped the girls cope with the difficulties, the girls were reacting to a problem beyond their control.

Chapter 5
Patterns of Divorce and Remarriage

Abstract This chapter assumes that due to the high frequency of divorce and remarriage in America, some people who seek counseling may be involved in complicated relationship networks. Visual displays of these networks in the form of affinographs may help find solutions through individual, couple, or family counseling. The network ideas, expressed through affinographs, can help counselors deal with problems related to the changing family relationships. The term *compound family* was introduced to differentiate between the nuclear and extended families from the complex structures referred to in the literature under a variety of labels.

The purpose of this chapter is to describe applications of affinographs for use in counseling and family life education. A professional counselor may require systemic thinking when there is a possibility that the clinical intervention depends on the understanding of the client's family. Family therapists routinely approach problems and seek solutions from a systemic perspective. Counselors also may find it advantageous to use systemic images (Dansereau et al. 1994) especially when their married clients remain permanently available.

In his 1964 book, *Family: Organization and Interaction,* Bernard Farber coined the phrase *permanent availability* to describe an emerging rule of marriage By the twenty-first century permanent availability became a reality:

> Each individual, at least theoretically, is permanently available as a potential mate to all other cross-sex individuals. An important point here is that being married does not restrict an individual with respect to his future potentiality as a mate in later marriages (Farber 1964, p. 109).

Shortly after Farber proclaimed his observation, demographers predicted that one third of all first marriages will end in divorce followed by about 75% of the divorced females and 83% of the divorced males remarrying within three years (Glick 1977; Norton and Glick 1976; Preston 1975). These predictions are a reality today. Among men and women born between 1925 and 1934, 11% of men and 12% of women married more than once (Kreider and Fields 2002; Kreider 2005). In the cohort born between 1945 and 1954, 22% of men and 23% of women were married more than once. Because most of the divorced people remarry, by the 1990s almost half of all marriages in America involved at least one previously married person (Wilson

D. Jedlicka, *Affinographs,* DOI 10.1007/978-1-4419-9395-3_5,

and Clarke 1992). These changes in family forms are associated with stressors and challenges for children and adults (Cherlin 2010, p. 397; Mason 2011).

Permanent availability of partners necessitates a dynamic theoretical framework suited for the study of serial marriages. Broderick (1972), Glick (1977), and Duberman (1977) noted that increasing numbers of previously married spouses had children in multiple marriages. The new theoretical framework, they argued, should include social and psychological links among the past and present spouses and their children. Bernard showed that even in the absence of face-to-face relations, and without children from previous marriages, mere awareness of ex-spouses can cause jealousy and feelings of competition in the current marriage (Bernard 1956, pp. 199–209). Add to this a widely accepted practice of cohabiting with people other than the future spouse, and we clearly have a situation where monogamy is no longer a norm (Smock and Manning 2010). To continue thinking of the American marriage system as "monogamous" minimizes the importance of the past relationships when they influence the quality of the present relationships.

The idea that spouses are tied to each other's past via their marital experiences led to the notion of networks in the study of marriage (Buric and Zecevic 1967; Noble 1973). A pioneering example of an analytic application of spousal involvement with social networks was Bott's 1957 study of a sample of London families. Bott found that interconnectedness of social networks of married couples was directly related to the segregation of marital roles. Her research prompted a number of studies all of which differentiated family types according to the network membership of each spouse (Aldous and Straus 1966; Minkovitz 1971; Salloway and Dillon 1973; Udry and Hall 1965). It is clear today that even a person marrying for the first time can become involved in a complex network of relationships via his or her spouse's previous marriages (Allen et al. 2001; Morrison and Ritualo 2000; Starbuck 2010, pp. 424–425; Wilson and Clarke 1992).

Even though people use the network notions when they define their own relationships, the dominant theoretical approaches seemed to be limited to the life-course perspective, socioemotional theory, intergenerational family solidarity, and feminist perspectives (Allen et al. 2000). Amato's (2000) review of divorce literature in the 1990s found that feminist theory, attachment theory, attribution theory, symbolic interactionism, systems theory, social capital theory, and the life-course perspective dominated the literature. Network theory, or its subset the graph theory, was absent. Even in the studies that seem to encompass network notions such as the multigenerational bonds after remarriage (Bengtson 2001), the analysis of changing marriage and family types (Cherlin 2005) and studies of remarriage itself (Coleman et al. 2000; De Graaf and Kalmijin 2003) have avoided applications of the network theory. This failure to rely on network thinking, when it seems to be a logical approach, has been an obstacle to moving beyond what Beer (1989) called unclear, undefined, and poorly understood family concepts.

To understand and define modern families requires the acknowledgment of the distinction between static and dynamic social networks. An affinograph uses the graph theory to accomplish such a differentiation. The dynamic families are distinct in that "(a) first-married and remarried families represent quite different systems of relationships; (b) there are different types of family systems in remarriage; (c) these systems have different consequences for component relationships in remarriage" (Hobart 1988, p. 660). The phrase *family system* includes both the static and the dynamic family networks. Families that include recoupling, are called *compound families.* This term refers to families that develop through accumulation of relationships within one generation.

The following discussion of the compound family is intended to differentiate the simple from the complex and the static from the dynamic families.

What Is a Compound Family?

A *compound family* is a network formed by two or more serial affinal relations linked through procreation or adoption. The simplest form of a compound family is a *double family.* Villeneuve-Gokalp (2000) defines the *double family* as stepfamilies linked to two-parent biological families through remarriage. The affinograph representations of families after remarriage reveal that the structure of a double family varies. Figure 5.1a represents a family with one remarried spouse. Figure 5.1b shows both spouses remarrying after their divorce. The letter *c* stands for "*children.*" If there are no children, the value of "*c*" is 0. Let us assume that children will remain with one parent and that only parents will have custodial rights after divorce. With these assumptions, there are seventy-two types of "*double families.*" This number of family types is obtained by multiplying the number of states in each of the four remarriage variables.

The remarriage variables and their states are: Variable 1, were there any children in marriage one? This variable has two states, yes or no. Variable 2, who remarried? Three states, ex-wife, ex-husband, both. Variable 3, where did the children from

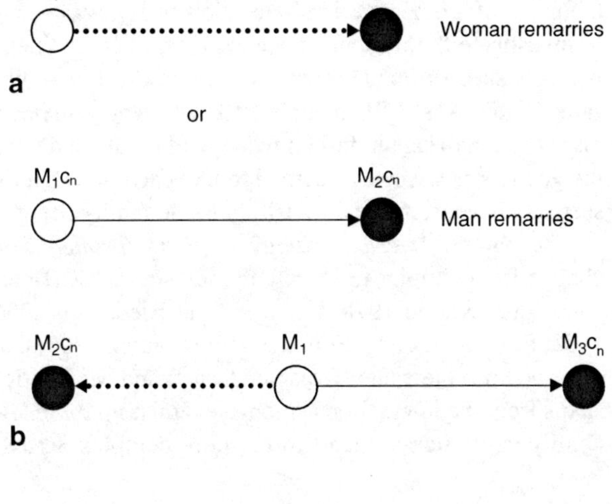

Fig. 5.1 Double-family systems of remarriage. **a** Only one parent remarries. **b** Both parents remarry

marriage one go? Three more states. They could go with their mother, or father. The third state is "not applicable" if there were no children in the first marriage.

Variable 4, are there children in marriage two? Four states of this variable include either one or the other ex-spouse with children since the divorce, both with children, or neither with children since the divorce.

A *double family* in any of its manifestations is structurally the simplest form of a compound family. Triple, quadruple, quintuple, or higher number of linked families is commonplace. Recognizing the importance of the new family forms, some family life educators use genograms to illustrate what they call "*blended families*" and "*binuclear*" families (Starbuck 2010, p. 3; Strong et al. 2001, p. 554; Williams et al. 2006, p. 514). Various definitions of the "*blended family*" tend to exclude indirect connections among significant others (as they relate to children). The following definition, for example, is typical: "If the children live with their mother and her new husband, they would be members of a stepfamily. This is also called a *blended* or *reconstituted* family" (Starbuck 2010, p. 3). It appears that such restrictive language conforms to the methodological constraints imposed by the use of genograms, even though network concepts are clearly demanded by the nature of the behavior and the resulting social structures.

The reality is that spouses can be linked through the children they had in common, through economic interests, through continued awareness of the past, and through children's attachment to current or previous spouses of either parent. Psychological implications for adults in counseling can also involve issues associated with the perception of the actors in the social network. Given these realities, the theory and methods of imaging family constellations demand a level of generality to account for family variations in the United States and globally (Ingoldsby and Smith 2006).

The variations in family structures in the United States are likely to be relevant to counselors. As a counselor, I encountered spouses who never discontinued their relationships with their exspouse even when children or previous economic arrangements were not involved. Sometimes these relationships were in secret, other times they were much like an episode of Colombo, "A Blueprint for Murder." Colombo, the name of a detective in a television series, was summoned by Mrs. Williamson to investigate the disappearance of her husband. When Colombo found Mrs. Williamson, she informed him that she did not call the police. "It must be Goldie," she said. Goldie was Williamson's first wife who remained a close friend throughout his second marriage in full knowledge of his second wife. In fact, the ex-spouse and the younger new spouse seemed to like each other. In this case, the popular culture seems to have captured a transition in the family life in America.

The phrase *American family is going through a transition* usually means a change from simpler to more complex structures (Bengtson 2001; DeGeneva and Rice 2002; Kando 1978; Lamanna and Riedmann 2006; Madhubuti 1990; Sadler 1988; Price et al. 2000; Skolnick and Skolnick 2007).Complex structures tend to be stressors of remarriage (Crosbie-Burnett and McClintic 2000). A common stressor stems from the interactions among several households (Manning and Smock 2000). Family constellations tend to be more complex across households depending on who is linked to whom (Lansford et al. 2001; Morrison and Ritualo 2000; Ruggles and Brower 2003; Teachman et al. 2000).

The level of stress during the transition to remarriage depends on the marital histories of at least three people. The simplest form of remarriage involves a person who was married before for the first time to someone who was never married before. This pattern of remarriage in which one ex-spouse is more likely to remain divorced may indicate gender, age, or socioeconomic inequality in mate selection (De Graaf and Kalmijin 2003; Jedlicka 1985). This form of remarriage is illustrated in Fig. 5.1a.

Figure 5.1 shows the simplest or what could be termed a "canonical form of remarriage." Even if there were no children from the first marriage, the attachment to the first spouse may vary from low attachment without face-to-face contacts to jealousy and obsession. The research on remarriage in general shows the importance of marital histories on the adjustment in the current marriage (Bernard 1956; Falke and Larson 2007; Ganong and Coleman 1989). Adjustment, it seems, is more difficult to attain if there is an imbalance in the social networks after divorce. The case below portrays an imbalance in a compound family.

Imbalanced Compound Families

An imbalance after a divorce occurs when one spouse remarries and the other one does not. Figure 5.2 illustrates an imbalance in three reproductive relationships between one female and two males. A person labeled *a dangling father* is alone after having helped raise a child, $c_{1,2,3}$ from his wife's nonmarital union N_1. The dangling father's own child is also with his ex-wife and her new husband, M_3. The subscripts show the history of the child's changing relationships with parents. Subscript 1 shows that the first child was born in a nonmarital relationship identified as N_1. Sub-

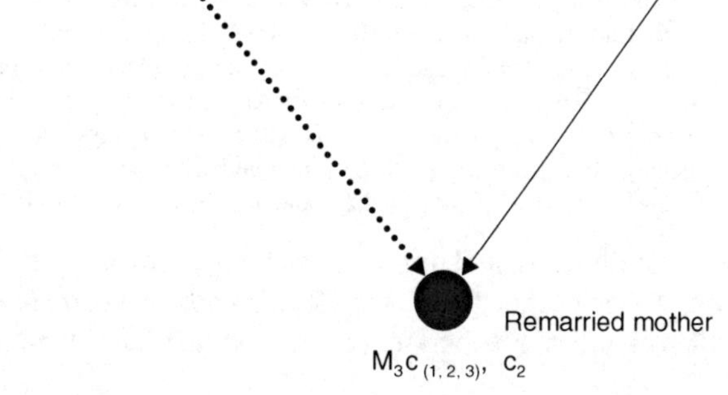

Fig. 5.2 A case of structural imbalance in a compound family

script 2 shows the marriage within which the second child was born, and subscript 3 indicates his mother's remarriage, M_3. After divorce from M_2, both children left with their mother who married the father of her first child.

Figure 5.2 shows an imbalance between the two linked households. One household, M_2, has a divorced male occupant. The other household, M_3, includes the divorced man's ex-wife, her second husband, and the two children mentioned above. The label *dangling father* expresses the imbalance verbally and Fig. 5.2 gives the imbalance a precise structure. Terms like *binuclear*, *reconstituted family*, *blended family*, *double family*, *custodial family*, *stepfamily*, or just *remarried family* fail to differentiate between balanced and imbalanced outcomes of serial relationships.

The imbalanced compound families can be equated to polygamy. For example, in polygamous cultures, a person can have children with more than one spouse. Similarly, in an imbalanced compound family, a person can have children with more than one partner, albeit not at the same time. Through the accumulation of serial partners, at least three sets of relations can be present in compound families and polygamous families. These relations include: (1) ex-spouses, as in the case of child support or alimony; (2) the relation between half siblings or unrelated children; and (3) the relation between children and the spouses who are not their biological parents.

The theoretical constructs presented in Fig. 5.1 are the building blocks of compound families. The following examples show some typical compound family forms found in twenty-first century America.

A Case of a Quintuple Compound Family

Let us illustrate the structure of a compound family selected from my observations in everyday life. One does not have to be a mental health professional to observe complicated family structures in their own life or in the lives of those around them. Compound families abound. The affinograph in Fig. 5.3 represents a family known to me through my acquaintance with a married couple, Jane and Geno (M_9). The narrative of this family involves the following participants:

> Jane and Jeff married for the first time and had one child, Martha. They divorced, and each remarried. Jeff married Laura, who had never been married before. Jeff and Laura had two children, Justin and Jamie. Laura died shortly after the birth of their second son. Jeff remained single. Jane married Tony, who was divorced from Lucy with whom he had son, Josh. Lucy remarried, and Josh moved with his mother and her new husband. Lucy and her second husband had a daughter. Jane gave birth to Matt while married to Tony. Tony and Jane divorced. After their divorce, Tony remarried two more times but never had another child. Jane married for the third time. This time to a divorced man, Geno who had three sons, Bobby, John, and Ed. All three sons lived with their mother and their stepfather. Martha, and Matt lived with their mother Jane and their stepfather Geno.

This family consisted of five households, shown in Fig. 5.3 as M_3, M_4, M_7, M_9, and M_{10}. To the best of Jane's and Geno's knowledge, no one in this family experienced bitter divorces, retributions, or even cutoff other than natural attrition of relation-

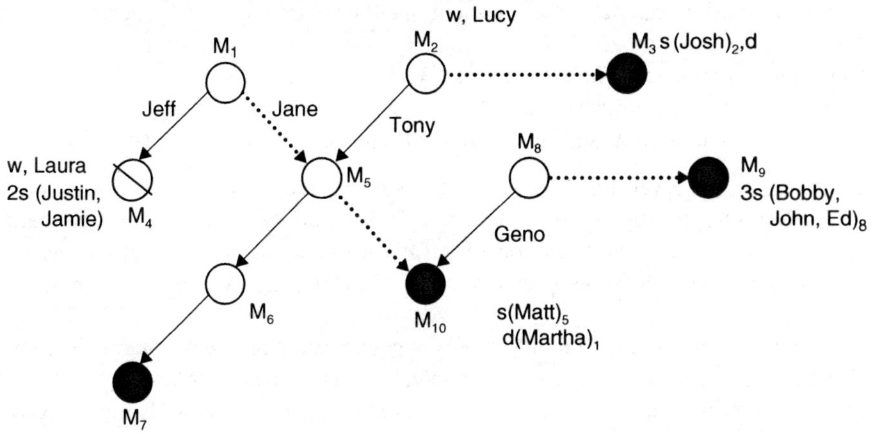

Fig. 5.3 A case of a quintuple compound family. The five linked households are M_3, M_4, M_7, M_9, and M_{10}. *w* = wife

ships when people do not have a reason to interact. This family consisted of five households connected through Jane, Matt, and Geno's children. Martha maintained a relationship with her biological father and with Tony. She spent more time during her formative years with Tony than she did with her biological father or Geno. Matt also maintained contact with his biological father Tony and his three stepbrothers Bobby, John, and Ed.

Even though this family did not seem to have issues requiring counseling to help with their relationships, it is easy to imagine that a counselor could encounter a compound family with unresolved and entangled relationships. Using the narrative alone to track "who is who" in such a family may be cumbersome without a visual aid.

An affinograph, used as a visual aid, requires a conversion from the narrative to the geometric and algebraic symbols. The above narrative reveals that every child was born to married parents. Hence, each relationship will be identified with a capital letter "M." As explained elsewhere, the subscripts associated with children will indicate the relationship during which each child was born. It is also convenient to note that there is no need to identify households separately from the marital relationships, because each current and past relationship is conterminous with a different household.

Each of the 10 marital relationships described in the narrative is converted to algebraic symbols as follows:

Jane and Jeff married:	M_1
Tony's first marriage:	M_2
Tony had a son, Josh, who lived with his remarried mother and a half-sister:	$M_3\ d_3\ s_2$
Jeff married Laura. They had two children, Justin and Jamie. This was Laura's only marriage. Laura died:	M_4 2s
Jane married Tony, they had a son, Matt. They divorced:	M_5

Tony remarried twice and had no children in either marriage:	M_6 and M_7
Geno was divorced:	M_8
Geno's wife remarried. Their three sons (Bobby, John, and Ed) stayed with their mother:	M_9 $3s_8$
Jane married Geno. Matt and Martha live with them:	M_{10} d_1 s_5

To an outside observer it may appear that having contacts with parents and siblings in five households may be unmanageable. Yet this family seemed to look forward to continuing each of their relationships. Of course, when I draw on my observations of compound families encountered in clinical settings, the picture is quite different.

One type of a compound family involves cohabitation and remarriage. The family structure of one case selected from clinical observations illustrates the flexibility of an affinograph to assist a counselor in visualizing the relevant family interactions.

A Case of a Quadruple Family Involving Remarriage and Cohabitation

Below is an account of a relationship experienced by Amy, a thirty-three-year-old client in a counseling clinic. Amy had personal issues ranging from guilt, jealousy, and proclivity to use illegal drugs. Her case illustrates the potential for using affinographs for counseling interventions. The narrative focuses on the relationships that may have generated some deeper psychic disturbances.

> Amy, now thirty-three years old, eloped with Lance, both at age 18 right after graduating from high school. Five months into their cohabitation, their daughter Alicia was born. Within a year Lance left Amy and cohabited with Miri. Lance and Miri had two children, a son and a daughter, before they married. Lance never supported Alicia financially, but he did keep in touch with her over the years. Amy raised Alicia mostly on her own for about five years. She then married Mike (38), and gave birth to their son Victor. Their marriage did not last, but Mike was a good father to Alicia and to Victor. Mike remarried Bertha and helped Amy financially. He maintained connection with Alicia and Victor. Mike stopped financial help when Amy formed a cohabiting relationship with Randall, a thirty-five-year-old divorced man who had a son, Allen, in a previous marriage. Randall's ex-wife, Marge, remarried Randall's friend Larry and became Allen's custodial parent.

This narrative describes three past and four ongoing relationships. Figure 5.4 shows this quadruple, compound family using an algebraic symbol for each relationship as follows:

Amy and Lance cohabit, daughter Alicia:	N_1
Lance cohabits with Miri, marries later:	$(NM)_2$ d, s
Amy marries Mike, son Victor:	M_3
Randall's first marriage, son Allen:	M_4
Mike marries Bertha:	M_5
Amy cohabits with Randall. Alicia and Victor with them:	N_6 d_1 s_3
Randall's exwife marries Larry and keeps son Allen:	M_7 s_4

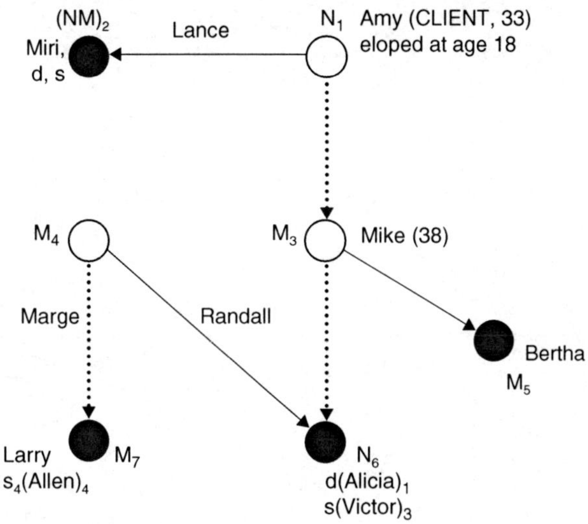

Fig. 5.4 A case of a quadruple family with interlocking nonmarital and marital relationships

This family consists of four interlocking households. Household $(NM)_2$ is linked to household N_6, because Lance is Alicia's biological father. However, Alicia is attached to Mike more than to her father; hence, they are also tied to household M_5. Mike accepts her as his daughter and keeps track of her as if she were his own child, Victor. Amy and Randall interact with the household M_7 to maintain connection with Randall's son Allen. This case illustrates that conventional terminology, such as *stepfamily* or *blended family* would fail to convey the intricacies of some commonly found compound families.

The compound families defined and discussed above have been restricted to the heterosexual families only. The next chapter will focus on the various types of family forms found among the same-gender couples.

Chapter 6
An Affinograph Method of Assessing Gay and Lesbian Families

Abstract It is common knowledge that gays and lesbians experience restrictions on their freedom to marry and introduce children into their families. The purpose of this chapter is to promote research and teaching of gay and lesbian family life. This chapter portrays the gay or lesbian couples within a larger family network that also includes heterosexual members of the family. Whether the heterosexual members are parents or grandparents, current spouses, or exspouses, affinographs show that heterosexuals are connected emotionally and socially with gay and lesbian family members. Affinograph images of these connections form a theoretical framework, which suggests that legalizing gay and lesbian marriages could improve the quality of marriage in general.

William Graham Sumner is credited with saying that mores can make anything right, and they can prevent condemnation of anything. Over centuries, mores have dictated the status of those attracted to the same gender. From ancient times to present, it is unlikely that there has ever been a culture all of whose members were heterosexuals (Eskridge 1993; Rowse 1997). The way each culture deals with sexual orientations varies from acceptance to intolerance. Prominent figures from ancient Greece and Rome, for example, accepted homosexuality as a way of life (Rowse 1997, p. 35). Medieval Genevans, on the other hand, were known to burn, drown, hang, or behead men convicted of sodomy (Naphy 2002). In 1779, the state of Virginia ratified a bill that would castrate men convicted of sodomy (Katz 1985, p. 24).

The remnants of oppressive mores in the United States continue through the belief that marriage is inherently "a union of man and woman, uniquely involving the procreation and rearing of children" (Hohengarten 1994, p. 1495), and that the same-gender marriage demeans heterosexual marriage (Warner 2004). These beliefs foster discrimination against same-gender couples who want to become adoptive parents (Kenyon et al. 2003; Strah 2003). They are stereotyped as unfit for parenting in spite of the evidence to the contrary (Taub 2007). "In fact, most studies indicate that gay fathers do not differ from heterosexual fathers in their ability to parent and to foster the healthy development of their children" (Armesto 2002, p. 74). Gays and lesbians are denied other rights and benefits afforded to the

D. Jedlicka, *Affinographs*, DOI 10.1007/978-1-4419-9395-3_6,

heterosexual spouses such as social security benefits, health insurance, marital tax rate, immigration law advantages, health benefits, and inheritance rights (Cahill 2004; Polikoff 1993).

In addition to these obvious conflicts between the heterosexual majority and the homosexual minority is a damaging bias embodied in the phrase "alternate life styles." This phrase implies that the people choose the gender to which they are attracted. If choosing one's sexual orientation were the predominant determinant of attraction, then everyone would have to decide whether they want to pair with the same or the different gender. Because it is not generally believed that choice is a determinant of heterosexual attractions, it is only logical to assume that choice is not the predominant reason for the same-gender attractions either. If it were a choice, everyone would be a bisexual from birth.

The predominant reason for pairing is not a choice of lifestyle but a search for love and attraction. Marriage brings benefits on the one hand and adjustment problems on the other, regardless of gender (Chambers 1996; Patterson 2006; Vanfraussen et al. 2003).The same-gender couples experience affection and conflict, satisfaction and discontent, benefits and costs. The major difference, and perhaps the only salient difference, is that gay and lesbian couples also must overcome socially imposed obstacles to a satisfying relationship.

Socially imposed obstacles might originate even within one's own family when the parents, for example, refuse to validate the sexual orientation of their own child. The affinograph method of assessment is quite revealing of family constellations and boundaries as they relate to the ego's gender orientation.

A Clinical Assessment Using Affinographs

An affinograph portrays families whether their constellations are socially approved or not. This bias-free approach has been particularly useful for assessing gay and lesbian couples and their families. Consider a case of a lesbian couple, Linda and Phyllis, who sought family therapy in 1999. Their family was not considered a "planned lesbian family" (Bos et al. 2004, 2008). Linda's son Jake was born in a heterosexual marriage shown in Fig. 6.1 as M_3. The empty circle indicates that M_3 ended in divorce. The divorce forced the issue of "coming out" for Linda. Adjusting to a relationship with children from heterosexual marriages and "coming out" at the same time complicated Linda's relationship with Phyllis, R_5, as one would expect based on the findings in the related literature (Cluines and Green 1993; Jensen 1974; Lippa 2007; Meezan and Rouch 2005).

At the time of the assessment, Linda's son Jake was eight years old. Jake's grandparents on both father's and mother's side of the family, M_1 and M_2 in Fig. 6.1, kept in touch with Jake. Through him they also had to interact with Linda. Linda's parents and her ex-husband's parents rejected Linda as long as she was in a relationship with the same-gender partner, R_5. Jake's father had custody of the child and the mother had visitation rights. The father objected to his mother's way of life and was

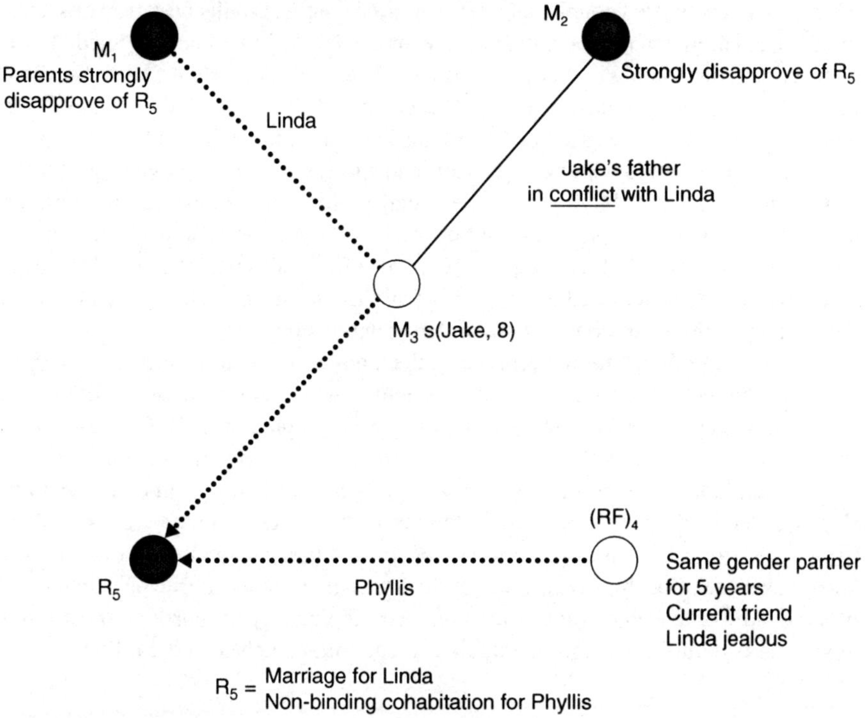

Fig. 6.1 An affinograph of a same-gender couple, R_5

reluctant to allow his eight-year-old son to see her. Phyllis, on the other hand, had little interest in relationships with either of their families.

A part of the conflict between Linda and Phyllis stemmed form Phyllis's friendly relation with her previous same-gender partner, $(RF)_4$. Phyllis lived with another woman for five years before they amicably broke the commitment and went in search of new partners. The letter F indicates that a committed relationship, R, became a friendship. Linda was jealous of this friendship to the point where she broke dishes in anger every month or two. They threw hard objects at each other that could cause injury. They also hit and pushed during arguments. Yet neither wanted to leave the relationship, because "the good times were more frequent than bad," and each was confident that the other will change.

Initially, their problems appeared similar to any other couple with jealousy issues. What made this case different and what distinguishes therapy of gay and lesbian couples from heterosexual couples is the ambiguity of the relationship status. Gay and lesbian couples, until recently and then only in some states, could not have a socially sanctioned relationship (Kramer 1997; Moats 2007). Some couples minimized this problem by joining a church that performs gay and lesbian wedding ceremonies.

Linda and Phyllis did not belong to such a church. They struggled to define their own relationship, but they never reached a consensus. Linda viewed their relationship as a marriage. She argued that because they live as a married couple and present themselves as a married couple, they are a married couple. Phyllis preferred less commitment and more interaction outside of the main relationship. Linda expected Phyllis to sever her friendship with her previous partner to the same extent that she severed her bonds from her ex-husband, M_3. She construed Phyllis's friendly relationship with her previous partner as a violation of marital commitment. In Linda's conception of marriage, one would not openly consort and spend time with a previous partner.

On the other hand, Phyllis took the social prohibition against gay and lesbian marriage as the guiding principle for her world view. Her attitude was, "If I cannot be married, why should I live as if I were married?" In absence of a socially recognized and legally sanctioned union, Phyllis and Linda struggled to derive their own definition, meaning, and boundaries of their relationship.

The affinograph in Fig. 6.1 represents the ambiguous relationship as a relationship R_5. Conventional methods of assessment usually require *a priori* definition of a relationship; otherwise, theories do not fit the graphic models. Because an affinograph is more abstract, it facilitates representation of both clients' perceptions.

Linda and Phyllis represent but one path from the family of origin to the relationship with the same-gender partner. A step in that path included a heterosexual marriage. That step is not unusual. In fact, social pressures channel everyone into the heterosexual relationships regardless of their sexual orientation. Because thousands of men and women succumb to such pressures, the quality of marriage in America in general is reduced through inevitable divorces, mismatches, and conflicts.

Gay and Lesbian Partners in Heterosexual Relationships

Barret and Robinson (1990, pp. 59–62) and Strah (2003) distinguish families with gay men who have been involved in heterosexual relationships from families of gay couples without such experiences. Cluines and Green (1993, pp. 117–125) make the same distinction among lesbians. A difficulty that homosexuals encounter deals with the issues of "coming out" and the secrecy that precedes it. This social problem is responsible for much individual suffering, divorce, and cutoffs within families.

The affinograph in Fig. 6.2 shows whether or not one's sexual orientation is kept a secret from the family, the spouse, or both. The families of origin are labeled M_1 through M_6. The word *secret* associated with the relationship symbols indicates that the gay husband (G) in M_7 keeps his sexual orientation a secret from his parents and his heterosexual spouse. The word *secret* in the relationship M_8 indicates that the lesbian spouse (L) is keeping her sexual orientation a secret from her spouse, while her parents are aware of her true sexual orientation. In the heterosexual relationship represented by M_9 a gay man and a lesbian woman are both aware of each other's sexual identity, but each is keeping that a secret from their parents.

Figure 6.2 represents a first step many gay and lesbians take before they "come out" and settle with an appropriate partner. In fact, some marry sexually incompatible partners out of social pressure. Others may deny their sexual orientation believing that through willpower and determination they can change.

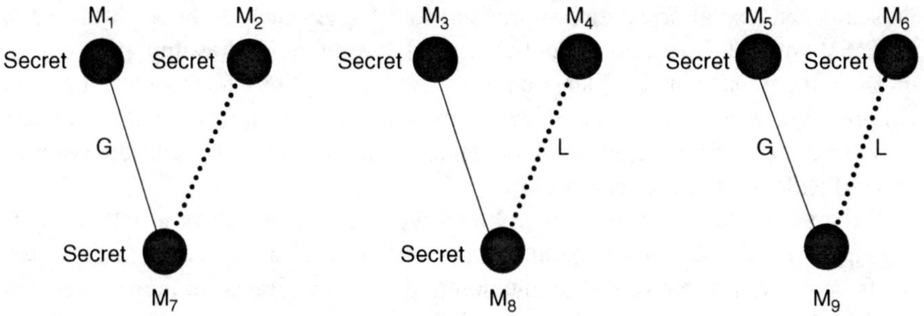

Fig. 6.2 Some variations on keeping sexual orientation a secret. *G* gay, *L* lesbian

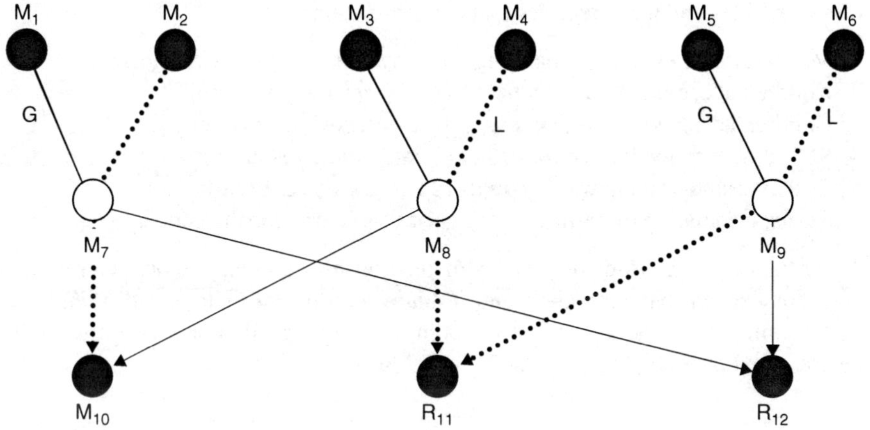

Fig. 6.3 A resolution of marital incompatibility through recoupling

Figure 6.3 shows paths to more compatible relationships than those shown in Fig. 6.2. Each incompatible marriage, M_7, M_8, and M_9, in Fig. 6.2 is an intervening relationship on the way to more compatible relationships such as M_{10}, R_{11}, and R_{12}. When adoption is difficult for the same-gender couples, intervening relationships become one way for them to have children.

Gay and Lesbian Families with Children

Strah (2003) classifies gay parents according to the method of adding children to the family. Some gay and lesbian couples have their own children from previous heterosexual relationships. Others seek surrogate parenthood or adopt children. Cluines and Green (1993) classify lesbian families as those who are "out" and those who are "not out." Barret and Robinson's (1990) classification is based on the marital status and sexual orientation of mothers and fathers such as those illustrated in Figs. 6.2 and 6.3. There is no doubt that each classification has important consequences for identifying problems and for seeking solutions for couples and their children. When children are involved, the extended family, the family of origin, and sometimes partners from other relationships constitute a family from the point of view of children in these relationships.

From the children's perspective, the relevant family members usually include grandparents. The fear of rejection by the family of origin sometimes keeps a parent from revealing true sexual orientation to their own parents. In therapy, secrecy can be a formidable issue when considering the influence of the family network on same-gender parents and their children. To illustrate, let us revisit the three types of relationships in Fig. 6.2. This simplest of categorizations still yields six crucial variables, each of which may be relevant in therapy and research. Below is a list of these variables and the categories that comprise them:

1. Marital status: married, cohabiting, or a casual encounter (3 categories)
2. Children accepted by father's parents (2 categories, yes or no)
3. Children accepted by mother's parents (2 categories, yes or no)
4. Sexual orientation known to partner (2 categories, yes or no)
5. Sexual orientation known to parents (2 categories yes or no)
6. Sexual orientation of partner (2 categories same or opposite gender)

This scheme yields 96 distinct states of relationships among couples with one or both homosexual partners. Gays and lesbians who reveal their sexual orientation face formidable barriers to adopt children, even though they are as nurturing as heterosexual parents (Armesto 2002; Taub 2007).

Open Adoption

In general, it is more difficult for gay and lesbian couples to adopt children than it is for heterosexual couples (Hawkins 2007; Mathews and Cramer 2006). One way to become a gay parent is through open adoption (Strah 2003). Figure 6.4 represents Sam Cruz, the oldest of three children raised in a close, middle-class family of Puerto Rican origin living in Bronx, M_1. Early in his twenties Sam formed a same-gender relationship R_4 with a partner who was not interested in adopting children. Their relationship ended, and Sam remained single. He was resolute to raise a child who would otherwise remain unloved and neglected.

Eventually, Sam adopted a six-year-old African-American boy whose biological father was in jail $(NA)_3$. Even though the father loathed relinquishing his parental rights, he agreed to the adoption as long as he could retain regular visitation. The mother, on the other hand, was declared incapable to care for her son. The affinograph in Fig. 6.4 shows the relationship history that led to the formation of a father–son household.

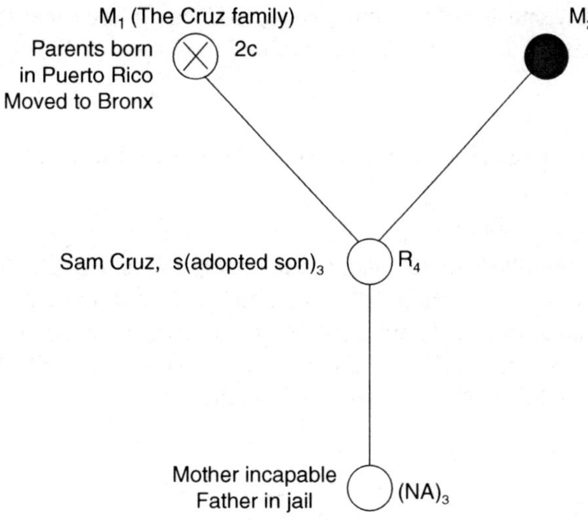

Fig. 6.4 Father-son household formed through an open adoption

Gay Father and Lesbian Mother

The family in Fig. 6.5 consists of two same-gender couples, Steve and Lonnie R_1, and Sue and Ann R_2. Both couples considered having children through artificial insemination. Sue wanted the child the most and arranged with Steve for artificial insemination. However, they could not find a clinic that would perform the procedure for a gay sperm donor. Because Steve and his partner had both been monogamous and healthy, Sue agreed to become pregnant through intercourse. They had a daughter in a four-parent-household. However, Ann and Lonnie left the relationship. For a while, Steve and Sue were a heterosexual couple, shown in Fig. 6.5 as a relation R_3.

Steve and Sue could not establish a sexually fulfilling relationship. Instead, Sue paired with Mary, forming a relationship R_4. Ann kept their daughter. Steve did not live with them. Nevertheless, he remained involved as a father in an amicable relationship with the mother and her new partner. Steve and Sue's experience typifies

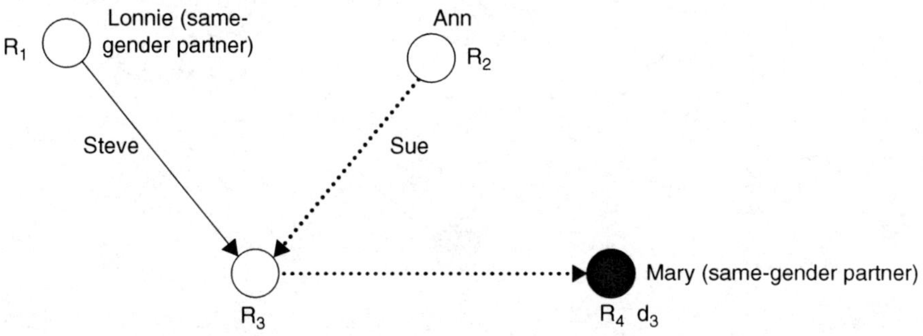

Fig. 6.5 Introducing children into a gay and a lesbian relationship

gay and lesbian parents who introduce children into their families either through intercourse or artificial insemination.

Stepfamilies with Gay or Lesbian Parents

A gay or lesbian parent in a heterosexual marriage who divorces and enters into a committed, same-gender relationship forms a stepfamily. The complexity of such relationships could be formidable. "A host of extra people and pressures push and tug at the stepfamily, making the determination of its own destiny difficult" (Einstein 1982, p. 7). An affinograph, however, can clarify and simplify a narrative that would otherwise remain incomprehensible.

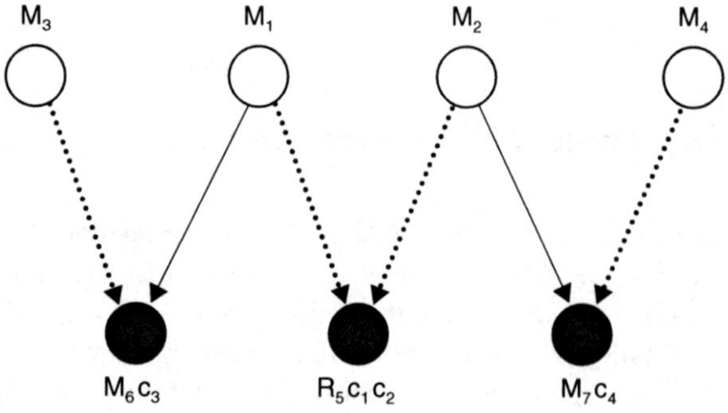

Fig. 6.6 A compound family formed through serial relationships among couples of various sexual orientations

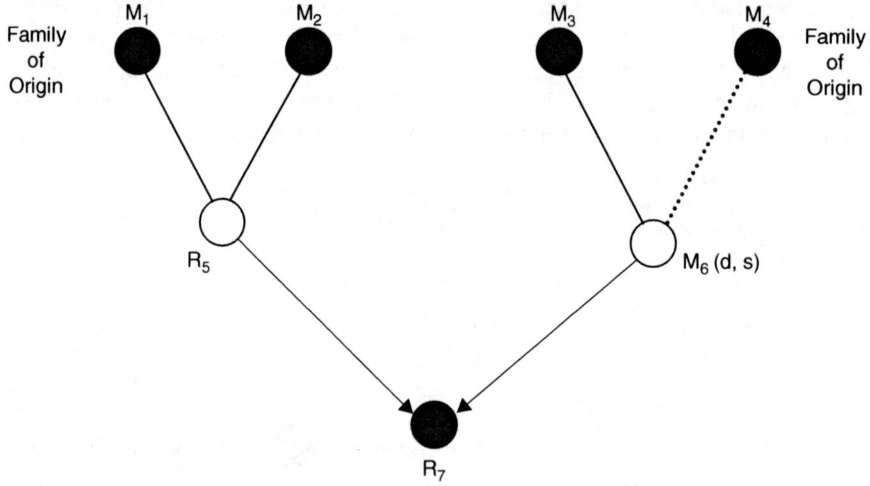

Fig. 6.7 Family constellation following the breakup of a same-gender and an opposite-gender relationship

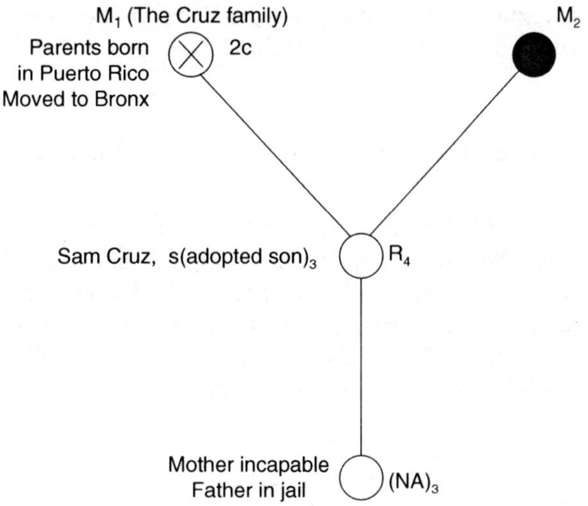

Fig. 6.4 Father-son household formed through an open adoption

Gay Father and Lesbian Mother

The family in Fig. 6.5 consists of two same-gender couples, Steve and Lonnie R_1, and Sue and Ann R_2. Both couples considered having children through artificial insemination. Sue wanted the child the most and arranged with Steve for artificial insemination. However, they could not find a clinic that would perform the procedure for a gay sperm donor. Because Steve and his partner had both been monogamous and healthy, Sue agreed to become pregnant through intercourse. They had a daughter in a four-parent-household. However, Ann and Lonnie left the relationship. For a while, Steve and Sue were a heterosexual couple, shown in Fig. 6.5 as a relation R_3.

Steve and Sue could not establish a sexually fulfilling relationship. Instead, Sue paired with Mary, forming a relationship R_4. Ann kept their daughter. Steve did not live with them. Nevertheless, he remained involved as a father in an amicable relationship with the mother and her new partner. Steve and Sue's experience typifies

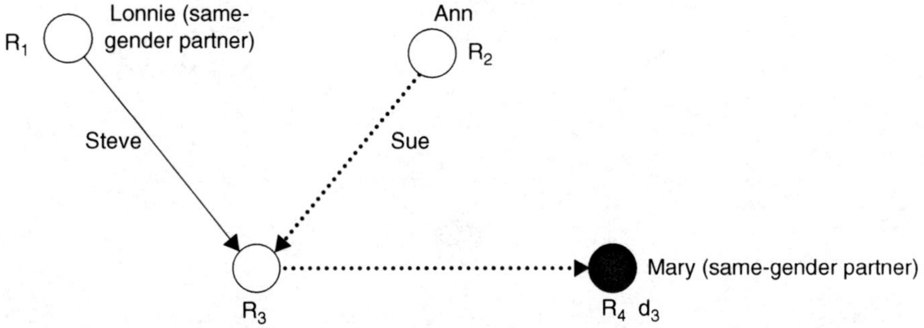

Fig. 6.5 Introducing children into a gay and a lesbian relationship

gay and lesbian parents who introduce children into their families either through intercourse or artificial insemination.

Stepfamilies with Gay or Lesbian Parents

A gay or lesbian parent in a heterosexual marriage who divorces and enters into a committed, same-gender relationship forms a stepfamily. The complexity of such relationships could be formidable. "A host of extra people and pressures push and tug at the stepfamily, making the determination of its own destiny difficult" (Einstein 1982, p. 7). An affinograph, however, can clarify and simplify a narrative that would otherwise remain incomprehensible.

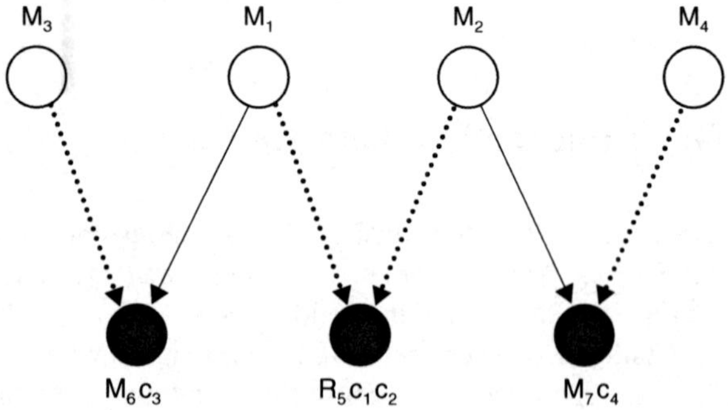

Fig. 6.6 A compound family formed through serial relationships among couples of various sexual orientations

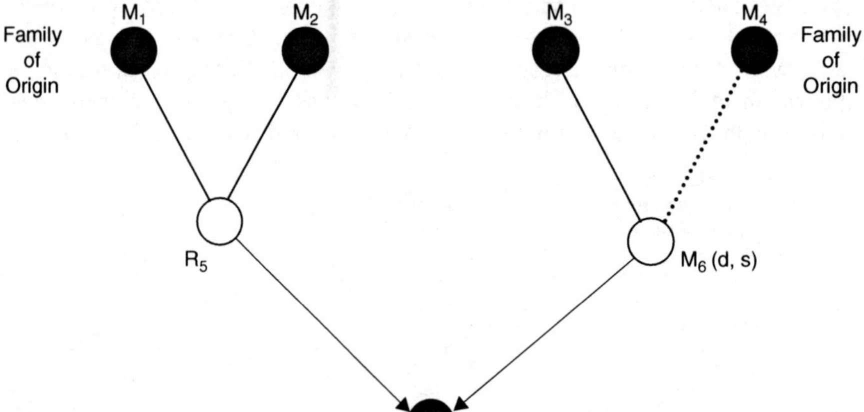

Fig. 6.7 Family constellation following the breakup of a same-gender and an opposite-gender relationship

Consider, for example, two lesbian mothers shown in Fig. 6.6 as previously married in relationships M_1 and M_2. These two divorced mothers formed a new relationship R_5. Their husbands remarried heterosexual, divorced women each of whom had a child, c_3 and c_4, from a previous marriage. One of the mothers in relationship R_5 is the stepmother to the child c_2. The mother whose child was born in M_2 is the stepmother to the child c_1. The subscripts indicate who is the stepparent and in which relationship each child was born. The affinograph appears symmetric and homogeneous with respect to marital histories of each couple.

Figure 6.7, on the other hand, shows a heterogeneous marital history. One partner in a current relationship R_7 is a step-parent who has never had children or lived with an opposite-gender partner. The step-parent, however, had a previous committed, same-gender relationship R_5. In contrast to the affinograph in Fig. 6.6, this family seems less complex but more asymmetric. Only one partner is involved with the ex-wife in terms of child support and visitation of children. Whether or not these variations in family structures influence childrearing practices and the quality of marriage in general remain to be researched.

Chapter 7
Affairs and Ephemeral Relations with Lasting Consequences

Abstract This chapter extends the notion of Farber's permanent availability to include couples in committed relationships who become sexually involved with others of either gender. Affairs have been a reality since antiquity. Depending on culture, affairs have been either accepted or punished. Today, in the United States the attitudes have softened, and some scholars even argue that infidelity has its benefits. In general, infidelity anywhere in the world tends to be more harmful to women. In the United States, affairs are often the main reason for termination of marriage, and they are a challenge for marital therapists. This chapter offers affinograph methods of assessment that can help researchers, teachers, and therapists visualize varied manifestations of parallel, sexual relations.

The mapping of affinal relationships would not be complete without accounting for extradyadic sexual affairs (Allen and Rhoades 2008). The word *extradyadic* includes affairs in committed relationships with or without marriage and for either gender. Affairs involving cohabiting heterosexuals, affairs involving homosexual unions, and affairs involving married couples are assumed to be a part of the social phenomenon known as *permanent availability* of partners. Even though Farber in 1981 applied the "permanent availability" concept to the "opposite sex" only, affinograph models include the same-gender affairs. "People remain in a state of readiness, with an emphasis on youthfulness, keeping attractive, and maintaining sociability" (Farber 1981, p. 203) whether they are in homosexual or heterosexual unions. Regardless of sexual orientation, people living in committed relationships become involved in affairs even when they are closely associated with religious institutions that strictly prohibit such behavior (Paine 2005; Thoburn and Whitman 2004). In general, people have affairs with those who may provide something better or different from their current partner (DeMaris 2009; Glass and Wright 1992; Previti 2004).

The word *affair* may not conjure the image of serious infraction, as the word "adultery" does (Lawson 1988). The word *affair* covers a variety of attitudes regarding parallel sexual relations. The appeal of another man or another woman can be stronger than inhibitions induced by morality, religion, (Paine 2005; Scheinkman 2005; Thoburn and Whitman 2004), or adverse effects on children (Flanagan 2009).

D. Jedlicka, *Affinographs*, DOI 10.1007/978-1-4419-9395-3_7,

The duration of marriage also does not seem to change the propensity to engage in an affair (Li and Racine 2004). Given the universality and persistence of the appeal of another person's partner, let us examine some trends of this behavior.

From the Scarlet Letter to a Lifestyle

Puritans considered adultery a grave offense, and they punished transgressors accordingly. In almost all of the New England colonies, adultery was punishable by death. Court records indicate that several people were executed (Kephart and Jedlicka 1991, p. 70). By 1700, the death sentence seems to have been superseded by whipping, imprisonment, banishment, and branding. Puritans believed that branding was particularly effective as a deterrent and the "scarlet letter"—later made infamous by Hawthorne's book of the same name—occupied a permanent place in colonial history. Under the Acts of Laws of Connecticut, to take but one example, we read that

> Whosoever shell commit adultery with a Married Woman or one Betrothed to another Man, both of them shall be severely punished by whipping on the naked body, and stigmatized or burnt on the Forehead with the letter A, on a hot iron. (Kephart and Jedlicka 1991, p. 71)

In reality, the sanctions, then and now, are more severe against women than against men (Chang 1999; Jankowiak et al. 2002). Even in the United States, a double standard in social sanctions may account in part for continued differences in rates of affairs between husbands and wives. According to a 1992 University of Chicago survey, about 15% of wives and about 25% of husbands reported having had sex with someone outside of marriage (Laumann et al. 1994). Yet, among those filing for divorce, about 50% of husbands and 25% of wives file because of infidelity (Boteach 2002, p. 115; Lawson 1988; Staheli 1997).

A study covering fifty two countries revealed that in spite of the differences in rates of relationship infidelity, the psychological traits of men and women who engage in these relationships are remarkably similar (Schmitt 2004). People with personalities that allow them to betray their partners have many new opportunities on the Internet. The Internet seems to have minimized the influence of the double standard in extramarital relationships (Maheu and Subotnik 2001). Websites openly encourage married people to avail themselves of the opportunity to connect sexually outside of marriage (Cooper 1998; Durbin 2003; Whitty 2004). Married women dissatisfied with their partners have an equal opportunity to seek "discrete" relationships. One married woman claims "I went on Match.com and within minutes I saw a cute guy's picture, so I e-mailed him" (Gertler and Lopez 2005, p. 46). That evening they had an affair.

Surveys consistently reveal that at least 77% of Americans strongly disapprove of any sex outside of marriage (Christopher and Sprecher 2000). The remaining 23% of men and women do not seem predisposed against it. Whether they initiate their affairs through the Internet or through more traditional contacts, when discovered, their behavior can devastate their marriages and their children (Brown 1999; Hein 2000), can lead to violence (Weil and Winter 1993), and extreme emotional hurt. I doubt that there is a licensed marriage and family therapist in America who disagrees with Richard Taylor: "Sexual infidelity almost always inflicts a wound that is very slow to heal and may never heal at all" (Taylor 1997, p. 197).

Even ephemeral affairs can result in unwanted pregnancies, serious health problems (Center for Disease Control and Prevention 2008), and agony. When an affair becomes discovered, spouses tend to agonize over whether or not they can stay in a relationship (Scheinkman 2005; Smith 2005; Vaughan 1989). Sometimes a spouse involved in an affair may have already formed another committed relationship. This chapter will sort out various forms of affairs, make complex relationships more understandable, and visually present actual and theoretical manifestations of affairs within the context of family relationships.

Using Affinographs to Assess Affairs

Figure 7.1 shows four types of affairs as they change from ongoing to terminated relationships. Ongoing affairs can go on undiscovered for years. That would be the case in Fig. 7.1a. Figure 7.1b shows a committed relationship that has survived an affair. The empty circle shows that at some time during the committed relationship R, there was also an ongoing relationship O. Other pertinent information that could be included into an affinograph in this case would be how the relationship terminated. Was it discovered or did it end in secret?

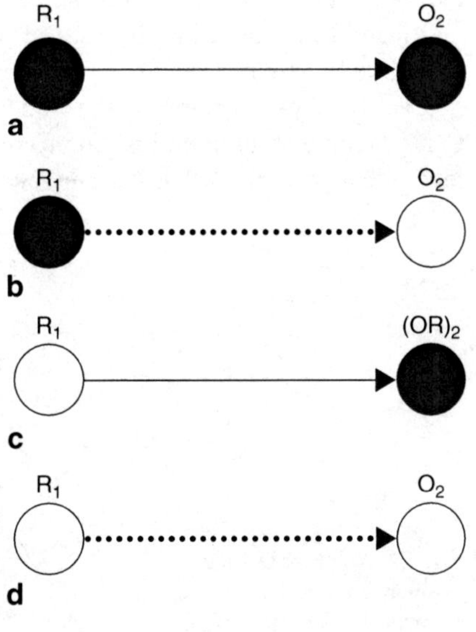

Fig. 7.1 Extradyadic affairs over time

Figure 7.1d shows that both the committed relationship and the affair had ended. Each of the structures in Fig. 7.1 can represent a variety of meanings of affairs including a beneficial side effect (Elmslie and Tebaldi 2008; Proffit 2005). Proffit (2005) describes the benefits of "infidelity" among Seychelles warblers as "a way for females to improve the genetic quality of their offspring." It could be argued that infidelity serves the same purpose across species, including humans.

Elmslie and Tebaldi (2008) identify a more direct benefit associated with human infidelity. They propose an economic motivation: Infidelity is beneficial if the happiness outside of marriage exceed the risk of getting caught. The couples who are most likely to claim that extradydic relations are beneficial do not use the term "infidelity" or "adultery." They use the term "open marriage." People engage in "open marriage" do not consider themselves unfaithful because they do it openly. They accept affairs as a part of their marital agreement (Block 2009; O'Neill and O'Neill 1972). Even in an open marriage, affairs tend to disrupt marital harmony (Bringle and Buunk 1991; Myers 1990).

Consider Fig. 7.2, a graphic account of McRay and Schwarz's (1990) marital history of a male who began his business career with the help of his first wife in marriage M_1. This marriage ended as soon as he discovered that his wife was having an affair, O_2, with one of his friends. He remarried, M_3, a woman who had her own career. They had their separate business lives and had little time to spend together. Even though his second wife was faithful, he became involved with Sabrina, designated in Fig. 7.2 as O_4. She worked for him in the same office building. He considered her a valuable employee. Because he wanted her to be more easily available, he rented an apartment for her near the office. Soon, sex with Sabrina became routine. His clandestine relation did not seem to interfere with his marriage.

Figure 7.2 shows each relation in a discrete-time sequence. These relationship sequences can also be constructed theoretically. Figure 7.3 is a theoretical model of the four expected patterns of affairs in two generations. In each case, the father in marriage M_1, engaged in a discovered affair. Fathers were selected, because they are more likely than mothers to engage in extradyadic relationships.

Case (a) shows a married man who had a daughter with a mistress in relationship O_2. An undirected dotted line connecting an affair O_2 with an affair O_4 indicates a theoretical prediction that his daughter is likely to become involved with a mar-

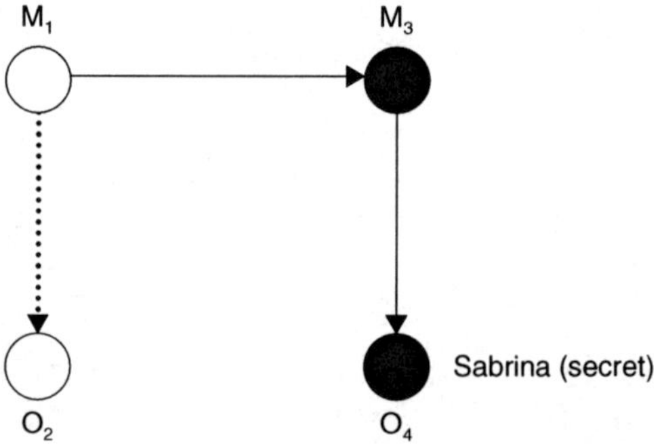

Fig. 7.2 An affair leading to divorce, remarriage, and a permanent clandestine affair

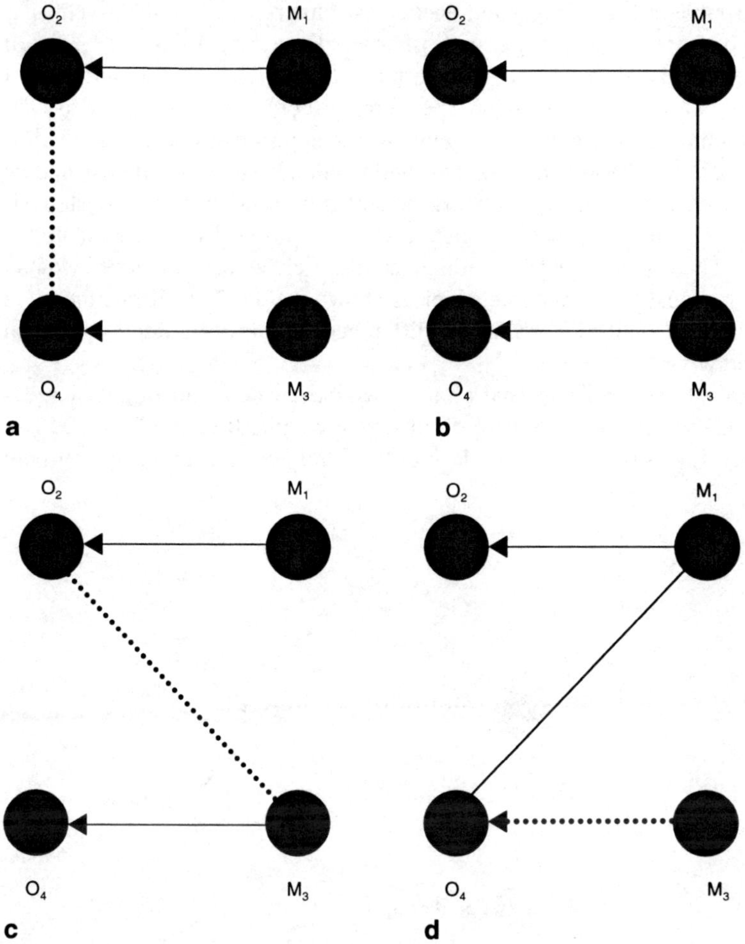

Fig. 7.3 Theoretically expected patterns of affairs in two generations

ried man, designated as an affair O_4. The theory is that mate selection patterns of children born to mistresses may become involved in affairs more frequently than expected by chance alone.

Figure 7.3b illustrates an alternative theoretical expectation that might apply to a male child whose father had an affair, O_2. The theory predicts that the son will leave his family of origin M_1, and marry, M_3. He is then expected to engage in an affair O_4 that parallels his father's behavior. One could similarly use affinographs to theorize about sexual behavior of the daughters whose parents experienced extramarital affairs.

Just like a parental role influences child development (Lamb 2004) and more specifically mate selection (Lazar and Guttmann 2005), family stories involving affairs construct the images of parents in the eyes of their children. These images may have a predictable influence on mate selection as some research on the psychoanalytic theory of mate selection suggests (Fisher and Greenberg 1996, pp. 129–130; Geher 2000; Jedlicka 1980, 1984). Affinographs in Figs. 7.3c and d show expected affairs based on the father's behavior. The daughter born to a mistress is expected to marry someone like her father. Theoretically, the opposite-sex parent is the ideal image. Hence, the probability that her husband would also have an affair would be higher than expected by chance alone. If the son is born in either relationship M_1 or O_2, the psychoanalytic theory predicts that he would be likely to emulate his father's role. The son is expected to initiate an affair either with a married woman (Fig. 7.3d) or repeat his father's behavior as shown in Fig. 7.3b. If this theory is correct, it could account for some of the differences in rates of infidelity between husbands and wives.

Some clinical cases indicate that affairs may indeed be a part of an intergenerational behavior. Consider the case of a married couple, Rita and Frank, M_{12} in Fig. 7.4. Their issues in therapy were lack of trust and jealousy. Looking over both

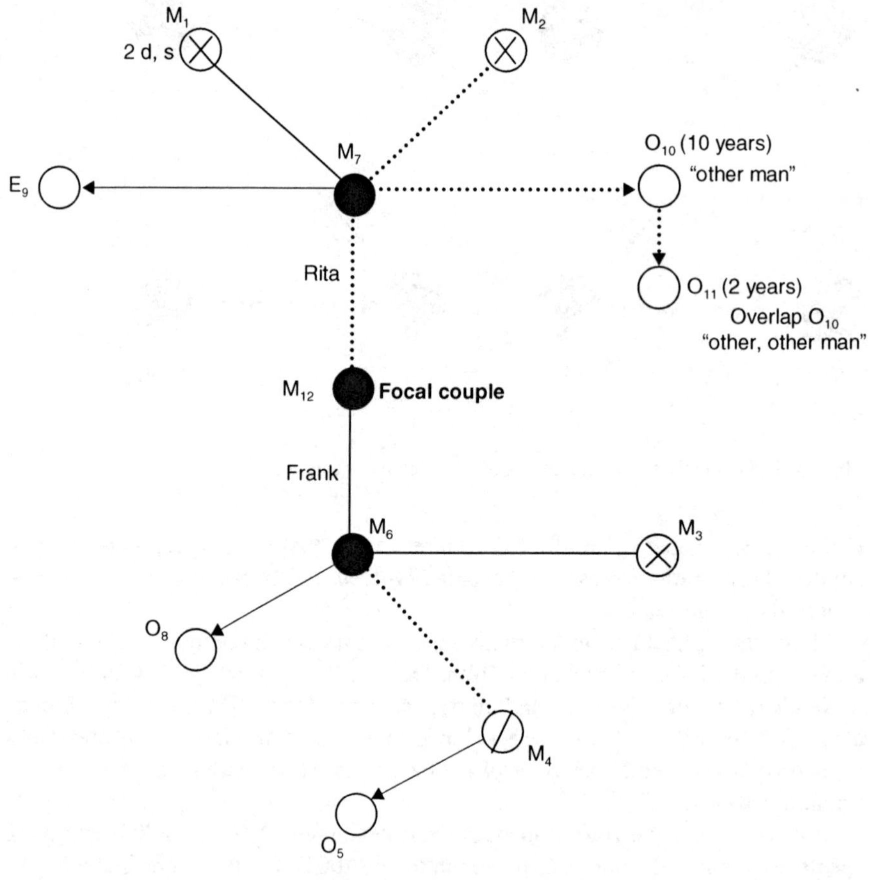

Fig. 7.4 Affairs in the family of origin

sides of the family, a possible source of their mutual mistrust could be found within their respective families of origin. Rita's father had an ephemeral affair, E_9, with a female coworker at the office. It happened on one occasion and would had been over had he not confessed to his wife. His wife was devastated but did not overreact. Three years later she became sexually involved with her husband's best friend. That affair, O_{10}, lasted about ten years before it was discovered. Toward the end of the affair, Rita's mother was also involved with what McGinnis (1981, p. 134) calls "another, other man." "Another other man" was also selected from among the husband's friends and is shown in Fig. 7.4 as affair O_{11}. When that affair was discovered, Rita's mother and father went through a painful reconciliation. Rita's father felt partially responsible, because he was the first in the family to take a sexual detour.

The lower part of Fig. 7.4 depicts Frank's family of origin, M_6. His father and his grandfather both carried on affairs for many years. These are shown in the affinograph as O_8 and O_5, respectively. His father's affair ended without a divorce but not without agony and counseling. The grandfather carried on an affair with his mistress for decades. His wife resented it but had no power to stop it. They were a wealthy family. In some wealthy American families, the husband considers it his privilege to have a "kept woman" on the side (Griffin 1999). His wife's anger and resentment fueled her revenge toward the end of her husband's life. He was in his early eighties, bedridden with crippling arthritis. His wife delayed moving him to a nursing home under the guise that she would "take care of him." Actually, his care was just enough to keep him alive and suffering. After a couple of years, Frank's grandfather was transferred to a nursing home where he died.

These experiences are traumatic for children of all ages. It is impossible to discern from any one case if the parents' affairs had anything to do with their children's mate selection. However, when Rita's and Frank's case is interpreted within the psychoanalytic theory of mate selection, it is difficult to dismiss their backgrounds as a mere coincidence.

Affairs as Risky Behaviors

It seems that many marriages are weak barriers to sexual encounters with others. Consider Jack, a 26-year-old, never-married tennis instructor who lived by his own rule of romance: maximum pleasure with no commitment. He would boast, "I go for the best-looking ones. They are all married." With his build, his smile, his wavy black hair, his well-toned muscles, and a "you can trust me" expression on his face, Jack was never short of female companionship, usually the married female.

Now let us consider the likelihood that Jack is a carrier of a sexually transmitted disease such as herpes, gonorrhea, Chlamydia, syphilis, or HIV. The Center for Disease Control (2008) estimates that each year about four million Americans become infected with Chlamydia, gonorrhea syphilis, or herpes. Considering that most of the STD infections occur under age thirty, the probability that Jack is infected is high.

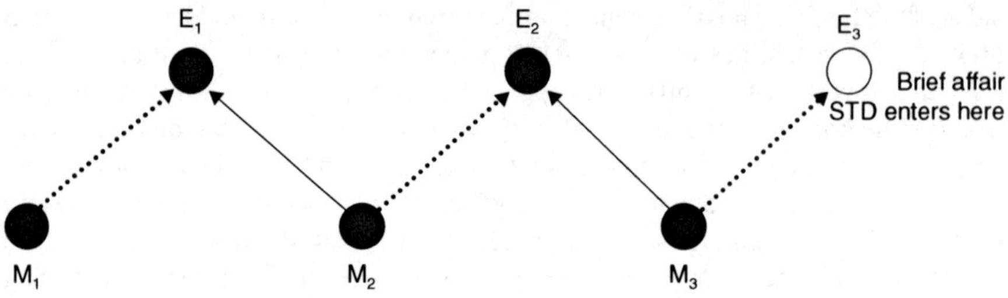

Fig. 7.5 An affair network illustrating the spread of sexually transmitted diseases (STD)

Extramarital affairs also place at risk the monogamous spouses. Even an afternoon dalliance can have health consequences for a number of people. Let us again use affinographs to model some theoretical possibilities of real-life behavior. Figure 7.5 shows a theoretical graph of couples participating in clandestine affairs. This figure represents a network of three marriages and three ephemeral affairs E_1, E_2, and E_3. The husband in M_1 is monogamous but he is not aware that his wife had intercourse with a married man M_2 whose wife also had an affair with another married man M_3. The wife of that man has been carrying on a noncommittal sexual encounter with Jack. Let us assume that Jack is a carrier of one of the more easily transmitted diseases such as genital herpes. With only one exposure per person, six married persons are at risk, including one who never strayed from strict monogamy.

The above scenario represents sexual affairs of heterosexual Americans. Committed gay and lesbian couples, as shown below, also engage in risky, extradyadic relationships.

Same-Gender Affairs

An affinograph represents affairs theoretically for any combination of dyadic and extradyadic relationships. Two models in Fig. 7.6 portray married heterosexual couples involved in homosexual extramarital relations. For men, such relations are as old as Western Civilization. It is a fact that homosexual liaisons among married men were an accepted part of life in ancient Greece (Guhl and Koner 1989; Kephart and Jedlicka 1991, p. 41). Rather, uncongenial relationships between Greek men and women at that time indicate a cultural predisposition toward homosexuality. Because Greeks subjugated their women, men often sought each other's company for intellectual and emotional support.

An affinograph can represent different types of affairs involving one or more homosexual encounters. Even though homosexual unions are not legally recognized in America, many same-gender couples go through a religious wedding ceremony and exchange vows for life-long commitment to one partner. These couples, just like heterosexual couples, can break their vows of fidelity through either a homosexual or a heterosexual affair.

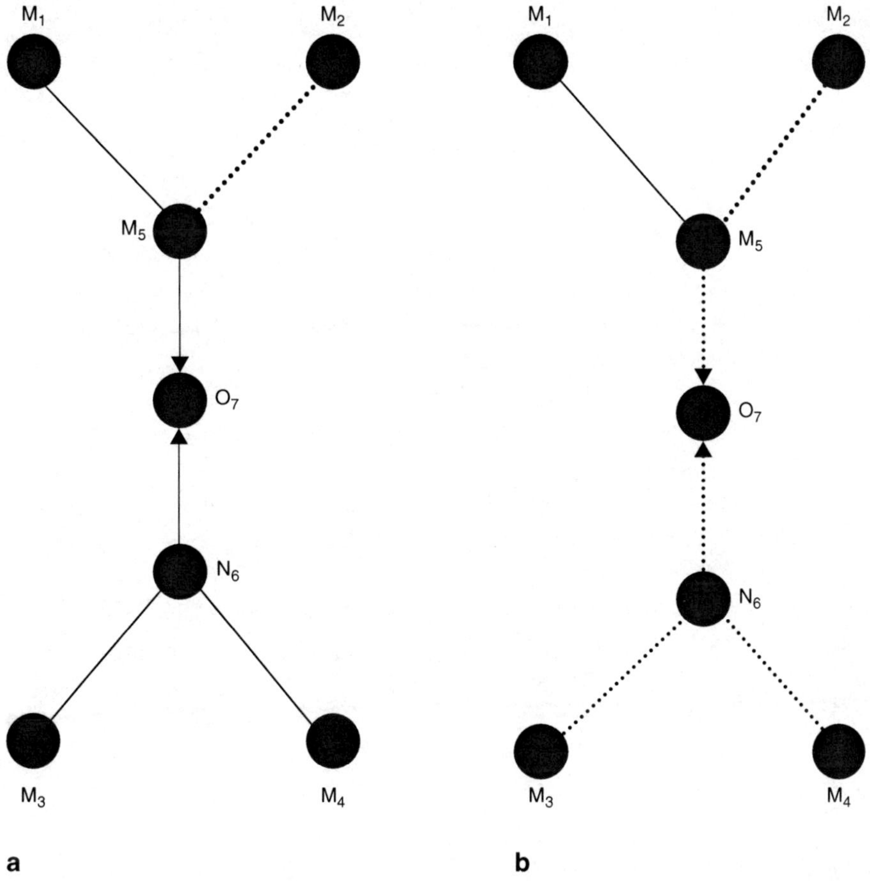

Fig. 7.6 Two ways of breaking the vows in one same-gender affair

Figure 7.6 illustrates sexual orientation of couples in reference to their respective families of origin, M_1 and M_2 for heterosexual couples and M_3 and M_4 for homosexual couples. In case (a), husband is engaged in a homosexual affair O_7 with a male who shares a committed relationship N_6. Case (b) shows the same pattern except that the wife is engaged in a homosexual affair O_7. According to Hughes et al. (2004), men in heterosexual relations are more likely to have affairs with the opposite sex, but women are less particular about the gender of their partner in infidelity. Some women, like men, restrict their affairs to the same-gender partners (Friedman and Forsyth 1994).

Various types of the same-gender and the opposite-gender affairs can be imaged using affinographs. A visual representation of affairs reveals whether or not an affair is clandestine or open, homosexual or heterosexual, long or short duration. An affair that each partner accepts is labeled "open." Using letters, directed lines, and circles an affinograph can extend the structural analysis of affairs and other relationships into family therapy assessment and interventions.

Chapter 8
Affinographs in Family Therapy

Abstract This chapter discusses when and how affinographs can improve assessment, tracking, diagnoses, and interventions in family therapy. One case illustrates how an affinograph helped shift the emotional focus from a four-year-old child to others in his family. In another case, affinographs facilitated didactic interventions. Through imaging a therapist clarified the family system themes that helped change the client's perceptions. In therapy with a couple who shared a dynamic family structure, the cumulative affinographs were used to track multiple presenting problems.

Today human society is very complex in its construction and is becoming rapidly more and more complex.

(Winfield Scott Hall, 1926)

Affinographs and other graphic images can be useful when the presenting problems lie within the family structure (Snider 1992, p. 80). On the other hand, imaging may not be appropriate in every case. Sometimes it is best to interact with a client immediately, directly, and without interference of any extraneous devices, including the affinograph.

Using an affinograph in therapy is not an *a priori* decision. Probably in every institutional setting in which family therapy takes place, each client is initially approached according to some routine protocol. These protocols may include questionnaires, agreements, and even initial family diagrams. The collected information, however, may not be beneficial to each client. A protocol tends to determine the nature of the relationship between the therapist and the client. Clients who could resolve their issues in one session may not have an opportunity to do so when a protocol is in the way (Talmon 1993). On the other hand, clients involved in a complicated network of past, present, and future relationships could benefit from affinograph-based interventions. Let us illustrate using actual cases when it is appropriate and when it is not appropriate to use imaging as a part of an intake assessment.

D. Jedlicka, *Affinographs,* DOI 10.1007/978-1-4419-9395-3_8,

To Use or Not to Use an Affinograph in Therapy

First, consider a case of a woman who walked into the clinic crying and sobbing. The intern on duty greeted her courteously as if she were someone visiting his home. He politely offered her a chair. As she took her seat, she muttered through her tears, “If I didn’t leave, he wouldn’t kill himself.” She wanted a counselor to help her deal with her guilt. The clinic required completing an intake questionnaire that would take more than thirty minutes. The rules required asking each question regardless of what the intern observed, felt, or learned about the client’s feelings, perceptions, and immediate needs. In this case, instead of following the rigid intake procedure, the intern employed a brief therapy technique based on Moshe Talmon’s book *Single Session Therapy* (Talmon 1990).

The woman talked for about five minutes. The intern interrupted her when she said,

“If I did not go to Houston, he would not have killed himself.”
“Where was he when you left?” asked the intern.
“I left him in Arlington because he was getting more and more violent.”
“Did he hit you?”
“Yes.”
“Describe to me in detail his violent behavior.”
She described this man’s mood shifts and details of hitting her and their child.
“I assume you took your child with you to Houston?”
“Yes,” she replied.
The intern shook her hand, and with all the conviction he could muster said,

“You saved your son’s life! Believe me. I study violent men. I can tell you that your husband would had killed your son and maybe you too. You did the smartest thing a caring mother could ever do for her child.” The intern reiterated, “You saved your son’s life!”

Her demeanor changed instantly. She sighed with relief. Another therapist stepped in trying to revert the client’s attention to the intake questionnaire. The client said, “I don’t need to come back. I understand now.” To the chagrin of the staff therapist, the intern reinforced their client’s new attitude and added, “From everything I know about cases like yours, you have nothing to feel guilty about. Only be proud and happy that you saved your son’s life.”

She left with a smile and many thanks. The whole session took about thirty minutes. The only information the intern obtained was the client’s name, address, and a telephone number. A week later during a follow-up telephone call, the intern learned that the client was free of guilt and thankful to the clinic for helping her. Had the intern followed the protocol without thinking, he would have filed several pages of information, prepared an elaborate genogram, and made an appointment with someone in the clinic in a week.

Of course, most problems are more complex and require a formal assessment. In general, early in the assessment process it becomes clear whether any family diagram may be required. If it seems that a family diagram would be helpful, the question is should it be an affinograph or a static diagram? When the presenting problem involves multiple relationships in various households, the affinograph may be the preferred model. I found affinographs to be particularly useful in cases with small children presented as identified patients. A therapist can use the affinograph to help parents shift their attention from a narrow focus on the child and look at the situation more broadly. The following case illustrates this shift of focus from the child to the family network.

A mother and her daughter Kate presented Kate's four-year-old son Bryce for therapy in a psychiatric, family counseling clinic. Kate and her mother believed that Bryce was mentally ill and were willing to commit the boy to a psychiatric hospital. These three clients resided in a trailer court, identified in Fig. 8.1 as a household H_7. No other person shared the residence with them. During the intake interview, I learned that Kate's mother and father divorced when Kate was twelve years old. This terminated relationship is represented in Fig. 8.1 as M_1. M_4 and M_3 indicate that both of Kate's parents remarried. Kate's father remarried first, M_3. His second wife brought with her two children, $2c_{2,}$ from her previous marriage M_2. Kate's mother divorced her second husband after three years of marriage. Kate married at age nineteen and had Bryce within a year. This marriage, M_5, did not last. After the divorce, Bryce's father moved to a nearby city where he cohabited with another woman. This relationship is shown as N_6. Bryce's father retained visitation rights and used them regularly.

The information in Fig. 8.1 was obtained during the first half of the first counseling session. There was enough information in this affinograph to challenge the notion that Bryce was mentally ill. We ex-plored past relationships and discovered that Kate's mother resented both of her ex-husbands. Kate joined with her mother in that resentment. In addition, Kate was reluctant to cooperate with Bryce's father to arrange for court-ordered child visitations. Another problem was an on-going conflict between the mother and the daughter. They argued daily. The tension between

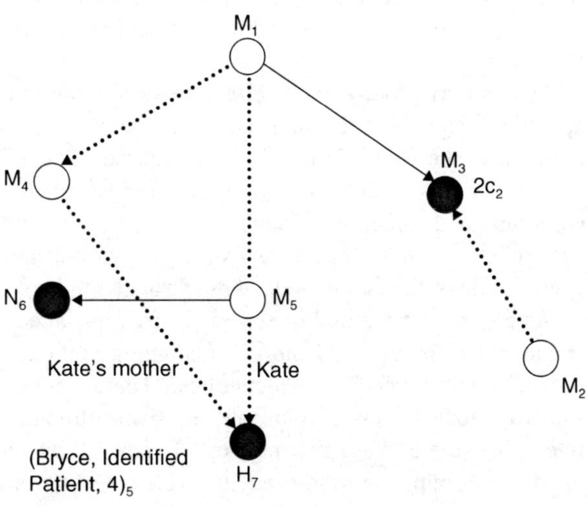

Fig. 8.1 An Affinograph of a family with a four-year-old "identified patient"

them was obvious even during the first session when they tried to give a favorable impression.

The affinograph helped visualize the situation and shift the focus from the child to the mother–daughter relations. With a move of a finger across the page, I could point to any one of the past and present relationships and simply ask them to talk about it. At a glance, the affinograph revealed each relevant household and the members within each household. I used their affinograph to shift the focus from the child to any other relation. Sharing the affinograph with the clients made them realize that Bryce was in the middle of a complicated emotional enmeshment. By the third session, the grandmother spontaneously expressed shame for ever considering hospitalization of her four-year-old grandson. Bryce's mother expressed the same sentiment. For the remaining three sessions, the mother and daughter focused primarily on themselves and their feelings toward their ex-husbands.

Using Affinographs for Didactic Interventions

The word *didactic* refers to a subcategory of the more general term *heuristic*. One definition of an affinograph is that it is a *heuristic device.* Heuristic devices efficiently convey ideas, understanding, and facts. The word *didactic* refers to a heuristic device that also produces a change in behavior, attitude, or emotions. An affinograph can sometimes serve as a didactic device in family therapy.

Some cases are so complex that without visual aids tracking and comprehending the family system may not be possible. Therapists are likely to encounter families that require an initial affinograph just to have a common reference to communicate with a client. Once the client and the therapist share the image of the family, it becomes possible to explore themes and contemplate changes. In the case that follows, a didactic method helped a client see herself in "relation between relations." Through awareness of relationships, she could gain a broader view of her presenting problems.

Jane, a thirty-five-year-old client, requested individual therapy in a family therapy clinic. She was twice married and twice divorced with one child in each of her marriages. She chose family therapy because of "her frustration and conflict with her mother." Even though Jane did not live with her mother, her mother provided emotional and sometimes financial help for her daughter. During the first session, Jane referred to herself as a "recovering alcoholic" and to her mother as a "reliable friend, and confidant who helped me through the hard times."

As a part of the initial interview, I assessed Jane's perception of her family of origin and of her marital history. I then inquired if any of the people in her past and present are also "recovering alcoholics." There were several. It appeared that an affinograph focusing on "alcoholism" may be useful in changing this client's perspective of her role in the family network. Figure 8.2 depicts each relevant relation and identifies each person who is an alcoholic or a recovering alcoholic.

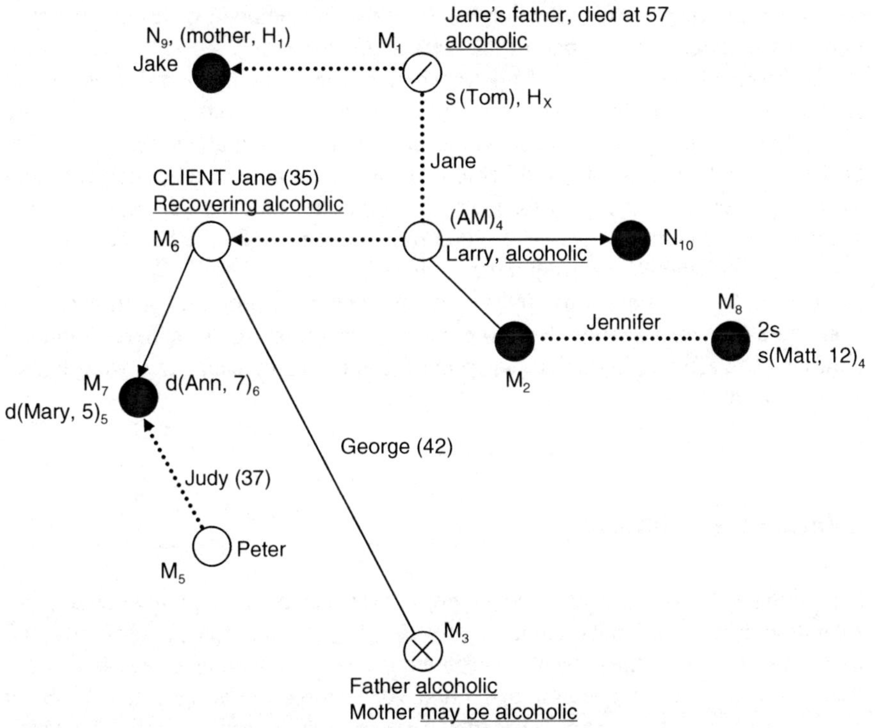

Fig. 8.2 An affinograph of relationships selected to shift client's focus

The affinograph in Fig. 8.2 shows Jane's family of origin, M_1. She has a brother, Tom, who is single, living in his own household, H_x, remote from Jane. Her father died at age fifty seven due to heavy drinking. Jane married Larry, $(AM)_4$, who was also an alcoholic. Their twelve-year-old son, Matt, was adopted by Larry's sister, Jennifer, and her husband, M_8, even though they had two of their own sons. Larry established a cohabiting relationship, N_{10}, and Jane remarried, M_6. George, her second husband, also came from an alcoholic family, M_3, but did not seem to have a drinking problem. Jane and George divorced after birth of their daughter, Ann. George remarried Judy, a thirty-seven-year-old divorcee who had a 5-year-old child, Mary, from a previous marriage, M_5. Her ex-husband, Pete, kept in touch with his daughter.

The affinograph in Fig. 8.2 served as a starting point for discussion about her mother's role in Jane's relation with alcohol. Her mother, now in her mid-fifties, found a companion, Jake N_9. Jane's mother visited and stayed with Jake frequently while keeping her own residence, H_1. Jane objected to this relationship on the grounds that Jake was taking advantage of her mother financially.

Jane knew much about Jake's marital history and his adult children. I deliberately curtailed the affinograph leaving out all leads to Jake's side of the family or his traits. This omission was a part of a didactic application of the affinograph. Heuristics dictate that one reveals the reality and understanding in the most efficient and parsimonious manner. This case illustrates a didactic method in which the information is used selectively as a part of the therapeutic process.

Jane noticed the omission of relationships in the affinograph and insisted that Jake's side of the family be included. I agreed to do it under one condition. I asked Jane, "Do you think your mother would mind your talking about her behind her back?" She did not know. I asked her to consult her mother and to invite her to join us next session. Jane returned for therapy without her mother. She explained that she preferred to continue therapy alone. From then on, we focused on her children and the people who were raising them for her.

Over the next ten sessions, Judy made demonstrable progress. With each session, there was less reactivity toward her mother and more focus on herself and her children. The affinograph helped keep the focus on relationships that were within Jane's control.

Cumulative Affinographs

Sometimes a family therapist encounters a case that requires simultaneous consideration of multiple traits, emotions, relationships, generations, households, and issues. In such cases, the presenting problem is just the beginning of a saga that unfolds unexpectedly from session to session. As each session brings a new problem and a new issue, a therapist may use the affinograph to link and expand the presenting problems. These expanded affinographs are called *cumulative.* To illustrate how affinographs expand through accumulation of new issues, let us describe, session by session, another case from a family therapy clinic.

First Session: Long-Lasting Grief

Bob (59) and Barbara (28), both in their second marriage, presented a problem, which they both agreed was due to Barbara's inability to overcome her father's death. She was seven years old when her father died. She claimed that she has been crying at least once every week ever since. In fact, what brought them to therapy was an increase of crying episodes. Some years after her father's death, her mother moved to another state and never remarried. Barbara's older sister married and remained in the same state and city in which their father was buried. At age twenty, Barbara married for the first time. Her husband was sixty years old. They moved to another state, where her husband died after three years of marriage. She claimed that during that marriage she still had weekly crying bouts in grief for her father. Bob and Barbara had been married for about four years and had a four-year-old son, Andrew. The affinograph in Fig. 8.3 depicts these relationships in regard to "grief" as the presenting problem.

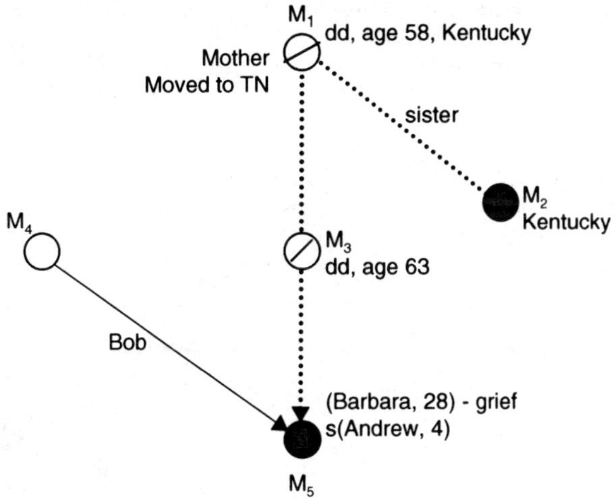

Fig. 8.3 An affinograph after the first therapy session. Focus on grief

The first session ended with an assigned homework. I prescribed *scheduled crying*. I also asked them to note on paper twice a day where they were and what they were doing when Barbara was not crying.

Second Session: More Grief Therapy

Barbara was still grieving, but she claimed to be less depressed. She did her homework by actually crying at prescribed times. The usual outcome of that homework is that a client tries to cry but somehow cannot. We discussed the control she had over her crying. The husband claimed that their communication was improving. The affinograph after the second session remained unchanged.

Third Session: A Secret Revealed

For the third session, Bob came alone. He said that during his wife's routine gynecological checkup, her gynecologist prescribed antidepressants to control the frequency of crying. The intake information indicated that this method of treatment did not work before. I secretly hypothesized that Barbara may be looking for an excuse to use drugs. I had an opportunity to test that hypothesis during future sessions and was convinced that the hypothesis was wrong.

Bob said that he actually wanted to come alone anyway. He felt that he was too old for his thirty-year-younger wife. He regretted leaving his first wife with whom he maintained friendship without sex. They have been seeing each other in restaurants and coffee shops during the midday only. "She has been my confidante and a

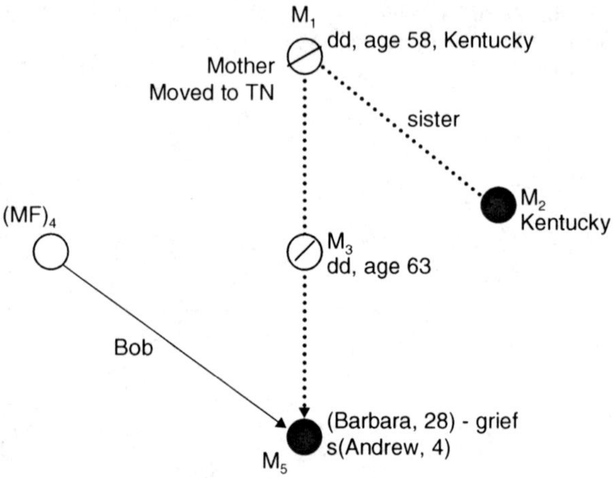

Fig. 8.4 Third session. Client reveals binding friendship with his former wife

friend. I can go back as if nothing has happened." Then, he quickly added, "Please do not say anything about this to Barbara."

I felt cornered into having to keep a secret. Bob asked for another session alone so that I could help him initiate separation. "To help me help you better next time, I must know exactly how you intend to raise Andrew after the divorce?" I sketched a hypothetical "post-separation affinograph" and pointed out various possibilities of post-separation arrangements.

The affinograph changed after this session. What used to be $M_{4,}$ Bob's previous marriage, now had a totally different meaning. That relation did not terminate. It changed from marriage to friendship, represented in Fig. 8.4 as $(MF)_4$.

Fourth Session: Intergenerational Cutoff and Conflict

Bob showed for the next session as scheduled. He decided that "divorce is out of the question" and that he wants to work out the problems with Barbara. This time he brought a new set of problems. He cried saying that his sons cut him off totally. His daughter would only talk to him on the telephone. All his children were angry and unforgiving of the way he left their mother. Both of his sons and his daughter were married M_6, M_7, and M_9 (Fig. 8.5). None of his children would let him visit or see his grandchildren. Lachrymose throughout the session, he lamented losing the love and respect of his children.

This case went on for sixteen weeks. Barbara returned to therapy with Bob for the last eight sessions. She engaged in some demanding grief rituals, which required travel, writing extensive letters to her deceased father, and more. Some rituals took place at her father's grave in another state. After a few weeks, Barbara seemed to have closed her grief process. She might have also sensed that Bob was more committed to the relationship than he was at the beginning of the therapy. In short,

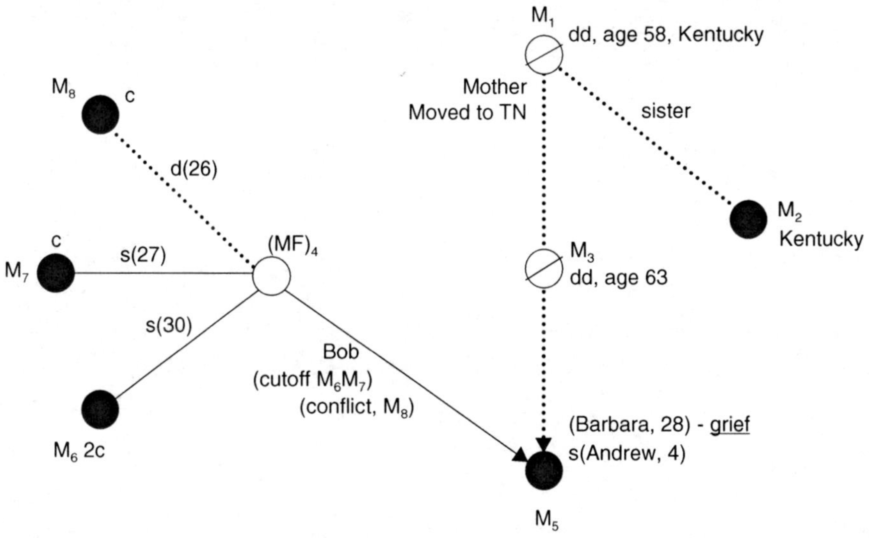

Fig. 8.5 Session four. The problem shifts to cutoff and conflict

the therapy seemed to have worked better for Barbara than the pills her doctor prescribed. Since the twelfth session she did not cry at all. She also began rebuilding her relationship with her mother and her sister.

Toward the end, therapy shifted from Barbara to Bob and his family. I never inquired about Bob's clandestine relation with his ex-wife. I speculated that the friendship was becoming more distant as Bob became closer to his daughter. Unlike his sons who lived out of state, his daughter was in the same town. She talked with her father more frequently, and Bob thought that "she was warming up to him." Both Bob and Barbara claimed that their communication had improved, conflict had reduced, and that absence of crying made them both happier.

Chapter 9
Affinology: The Affinograph Method for Genealogy

Abstract The word "affinology" is used instead of the conventional term, *genealogy* to include a wider range of relationships without regard for gender or pedigree. Four affinology charts are presented. One shows the lineage of two branches of an American colonial family. Another shows the descent of Hawaiian Queen Liliuokalani. Early polygamy among the Hawaiian monarchs is compared to marital histories of Elizabeth Taylor and Richard Burton. The fourth affinology depicts President Barack H. Obama's family. The affinograph of his family spans North America, Europe, Asia, and Africa through a network of strict monogamy, serial monogamy, and polygamy. President Obama's family history may be one of the most complex of all presidential families.

Genealogy, a study of ancestry and family history, could be viewed as the oldest form of social science. Genealogical records are found in ancient civilizations such as Egypt, Greece, and Rome. In Christianity, The Book of Genesis gives the genealogy of Christ. According to Potter-Phillips (1999), the origin of the "family tree" comes from the Isaiah 11:1 reference to Jesus Christ as being of the "tree of Jesse": "There shall come forth a rod out of the stem of Jesse, and a branch shall grow out of his roots." These ancient records of descent remained as narratives until family tree representations appeared in the ninth century (Freeman 2004, p. 21).

The word *genealogy* stems from the Greek word meaning "generations." Over the years, "genealogy" became synonymous with "pedigrees." The nineteenth-century eugenicists used genealogy to identify "distinguished ancestry" and "purity of breed." Today, these notions are antiquated. A more contemporary term suggested here is *affinology*. The word *affinology* could be defined as "a graphic account of the intergenerational and intragenerational dynamics of descent, procreation, adoption, and affinal union."

This definition has two advantages. One, it is free of connotations associated with the word "pedigree." Two, it avoids a bias toward consanguinity as the only way of descent. Affinology charts represent the same-gender unions and adoptions as a different path to family formation and intergenerational continuity. Rather than excluding or stigmatizing family forms, affinology charts apply across contemporary and ancient cultures.

D. Jedlicka, *Affinographs*, DOI 10.1007/978-1-4419-9395-3_9,

Four affinologies presented in this chapter cover ancient and modern families. The first affinology is of an Anglo-American family with roots in colonial New England. This family, under the pseudonym Kallikak, was scrutinized by eugenicists early in the twentieth century. Eugenicists compiled hundreds of Kallikak family records to contrast genetic traits of two branches of this family. The second affinology captures the dynamics of polygamy among the ancient Hawaiian elites. The third affinology depicts Elizabeth Taylor and Richard Burton. Their experiences show the similarity between serial monogamy today and polygamy in ancient Hawaii. The difference is that complex marital relationships occurred early during the monarchy and culminated in predominantly strict monogamy at the end of the nineteenth century. Taylor and Burton, on the other hand, descended from strictly monogamous generations and evolved into a complex family of serial marriages. Their lives and families have been of as much interest as if they were royalty (Bragg 1988; Cottrell and Cashin 1971; Heymann 1995; McGoldrick et al. 2008, p. 141; Jenkins 1993; Walker 1997, pp. 410–413).

The fourth affinology represents the family of the President of the United States, Barack Hussein Obama. His affinology illustrates an emerged family form. As immigrants from all continents integrate into the American society, they produce new family forms with networks that span the globe. President Obama's family network spans across Europe, North America, Africa, and Asia.

President Obama's family follows chronologically the colonial family types. It is befitting, therefore, to begin with the affinology of the Kallikak family. This family is presented first as a baseline for comparison and contrast with other forms of American families including the Hawaiian Royal Family, modern serial monogamy, and emerged families that span the globe.

Affinology of the Kallikak Family

Goddard (1912) coined the name Kallikak to protect the privacy of a family whose origin he defined as being "of good English blood" (Goddard 1912, p. 50). In his quest for hereditary traits, Goddard selected a family with a history of what today we would call "learning disabilities." Martin Kallikak, Sr., a descendent of Casper Kallikak who died in 1735 (Fig. 9.1), fathered an out-of-wedlock son, Martin Jr., with a learning-disabled woman. Martin Jr., also labeled learning disabled, married and had eight surviving children. Figure 9.2 portrays descendents of two of his children, Nathan and Sal. Children and partners with learning disabilities are identified with an "*". Goddard tracked descendents of each of these children and the descendents of each of the seven Martin Jr.'s half brothers and half sisters. His study found that in each generation, some descendents of Martin Jr. were learning disabled. No such disabilities were found among any descendent of his half brothers and half sisters. Figure 9.1 shows descendents of the longest-living son, Joseph, born within Martin Sr.'s marriage.

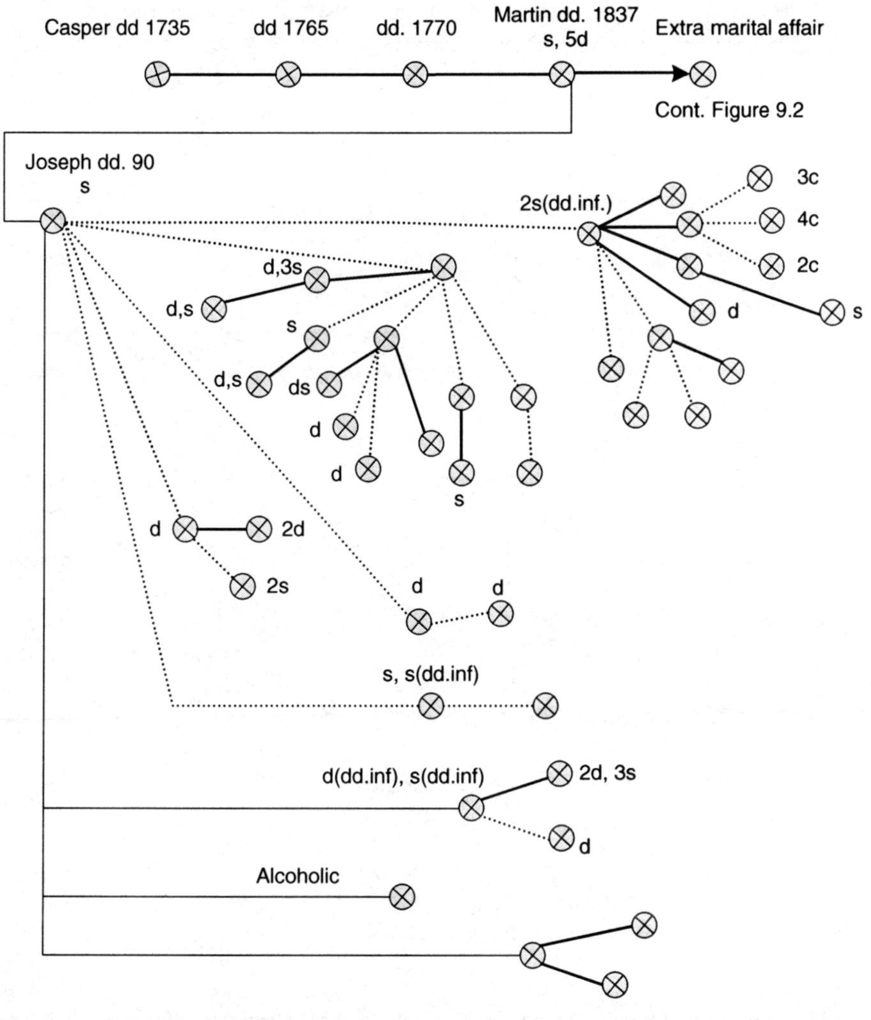

Fig. 9.1 A segment of Kallikak family tree stemming from legal marriage. *s* son, *d* daughter, *c* children unknown gender, *dd.* died, *inf.* infancy

An affinology distinguishes between two types of persons: those who never change their relationship status and those who do. A person who never changes a relationship does not reproduce, marry, or otherwise form a lasting affinal relationship. In an affinograph, such a person remains associated with the family of origin and is represented with the letters "d" for a daughter or "s" for a son. A person who changes marital status is represented with a solid line for a male or a dotted line for a female. Undirected lines are descent lines, and directed lines show changes within a generation. An asterisk "*" symbolizes a learning disability.

Figure 9.2 shows that learning disabilities may have a genetic origin. One branch of the family, Fig. 9.1, had no known learning disabilities. On the other

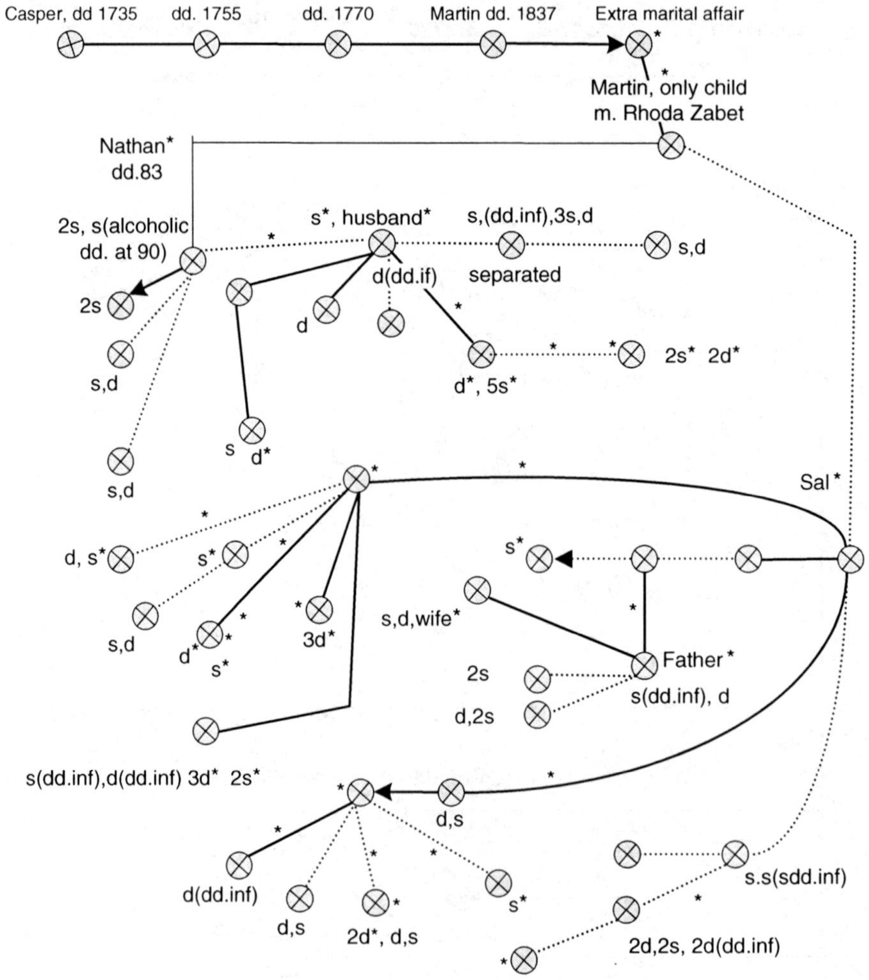

Fig. 9.2 A segment of Kallikak family tree stemming from an extramarital affair. *s* son, *d* daughter, *c* children unknown gender, *dd.* died, *inf.* infancy, * = a specific common trait

hand, the branch of the family started by the same male and a learning-disabled female accounted for disabilities in each of the subsequent seven generations. Figure 9.2 also reveals that descendents of Nathan and Sal, two of Martin Jr.'s eight children, selected eight partners with learning disabilities. Every instance of parenting with a learning-disabled person resulted in at least one child also being learning disabled.

Relationships on both sides of Kallikak family, Figs. 9.1 and 9.2, were quite stable. Only the descendents of Martin Jr., shown in Fig. 9.2, experienced serial relationships. The arrows in Fig. 9.2 indicate that in seven generations two males and one female divorced and remarried. Two of these remarriages were to a learning-disabled person, after a divorce from a learning-able person.

During the same time in history, in what is today the state of Hawaii, families were more complex and dynamic. Affinology chart for the last Hawaiian queen illustrates the family structures as they unraveled from the polygamy of the early nineteenth century to the strict monogamy at the end of the monarchy in 1890s.

The Lineage of Queen Liliuokalani

The affinology chart in Fig. 9.3 represents the royal lineage of Lydia Kamaka'eha, known as Queen Liliuokalani. Queen Liliuokalani, the last monarch of the Kingdom of Hawaii, was born September 2, 1838 on the island of Oahu. She reigned

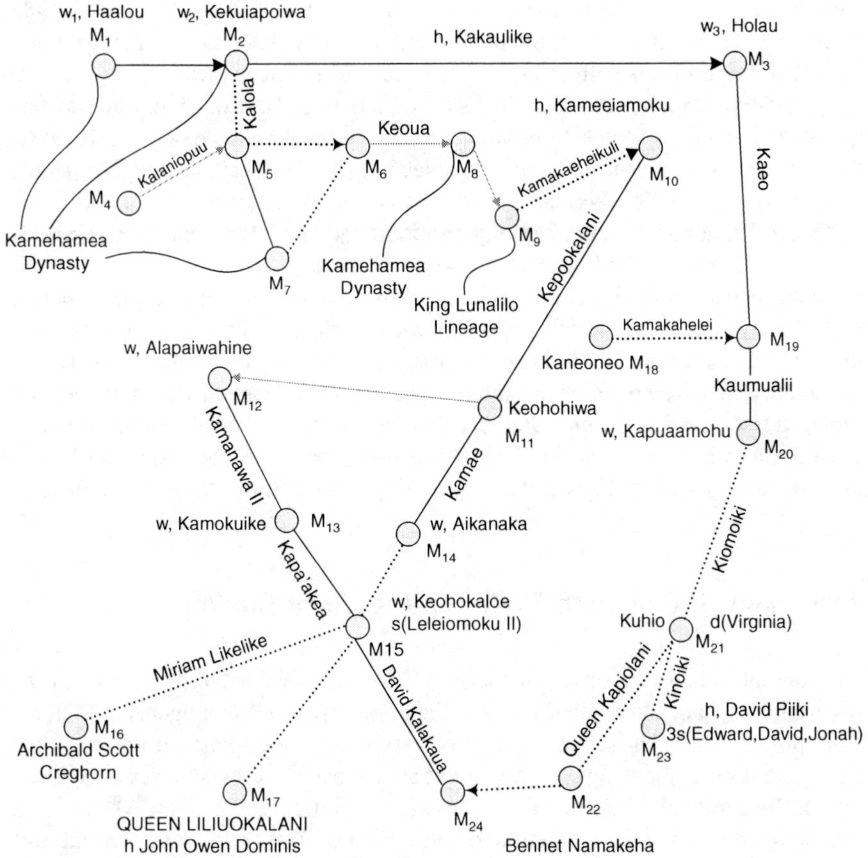

Fig. 9.3 The lineage of Queen Liliuokalani. The last monarch of The Kingdom of Hawaii. *h* husband, *w* wife

from 1891 until her abdication in 1893 (Liliuokalani 2007). In 1862, she married John Owen Dominis, the son of Captain John and Mary Dominis. Her father was Kapa'akea and mother Keohokaloe, M_{15}. According to the genealogical chart compiled by the Bishop Museum in Oahu, all of the Hawaiian dynasties shared a common origin. For example, Kakaulike's third wife Holau, $M_{3,}$ was a direct ancestor of Queen Kapiolani, the wife of King David Kalakaua, M_{24}, and the brother of Queen Liliuokalani (M_{17}). The Kamehamea dynasty and King Lunalilo dynasty also share a common ancestry through three marriages of Keoua M_6, M_8, and M_9. Keoua's third wife Kamakaeheikuli, M_{10}, was the mother of Liliuokalani's great grandfather, M_{11}.

Figure 9.3 also shows that Queen Lydia Liliuokalani's mother and father had the same grandfather, Kepookalani, who was born in the marriage M_{10} (M_{11} and M_{12}). His first wife Keohohiwa, M_{11}, was Keohokaloe's grandmother, M_{15}, and his second wife Alapaiwahine, M_{12}, was Kapa'akea's grandmother. Liliuokalani's brother David Kalakaua continued the royal tradition of marrying within the royal lineage. He married Kapiolani, the widow of high chief Bennet Namakeha, M_{22} (Allen 1982, p. 86). Lydia Liliuokalani, on the other hand, not only discontinued that tradition, but she married interracially. Her mother-in-law, Mary, never accepted Lydia as an appropriate wife for her son John. In his introduction to "Hawaii's Story by Hawaii's Queen," Glen Grant writes: "For twenty years Lydia Dominis quietly suffered the hostility of her mother-in-law, seeking solace in frequent visits among her people, lengthy stays on her Waikiki lands, and in music" (Liliuokalani 2007, p. IX).

Queen Liliuokalani never had any children, and she never remarried. Her husband, John Dominis, died in 1891, the year she became the queen. From age fifty three through seventy nine she lived alone until death in 1917. Her strictly monogamous lifestyle reflected the departure from the Hawaiian traditions and adaptation of the marriage codes brought to Hawaii during the British colonial rule. In the twentieth century, marriage patterns in Hawaii became more dynamic as serial monogamy replaced traditional polygamy (Jedlicka 1975a). In general, serial monogamy in the United States has produced families whose structures resemble traditional Hawaiian polygamy. An affinology of the modern day elites will illustrate this contention.

Affinology of Elizabeth Taylor and Richard Burton

Affinograph images of serial marriages in America reveal family structures that resemble polygamy in ancient Hawaii. Functionally, serial monogamy is different from polygamy in that sexual activity is restricted to one spouse at a time. Structurally, family relationships, even without sexual access to ex-spouses or partners, tend to be cumulative. Cumulative relations are particularly evident when parenting simultaneously with a current and an ex-partner. The children in such multiple households may live with stepbrothers and stepsisters who could legally marry each other. Because it is likely that some such marriages take place, serial monogamy may be closer to the ancient polygamy than to the strict monogamy.

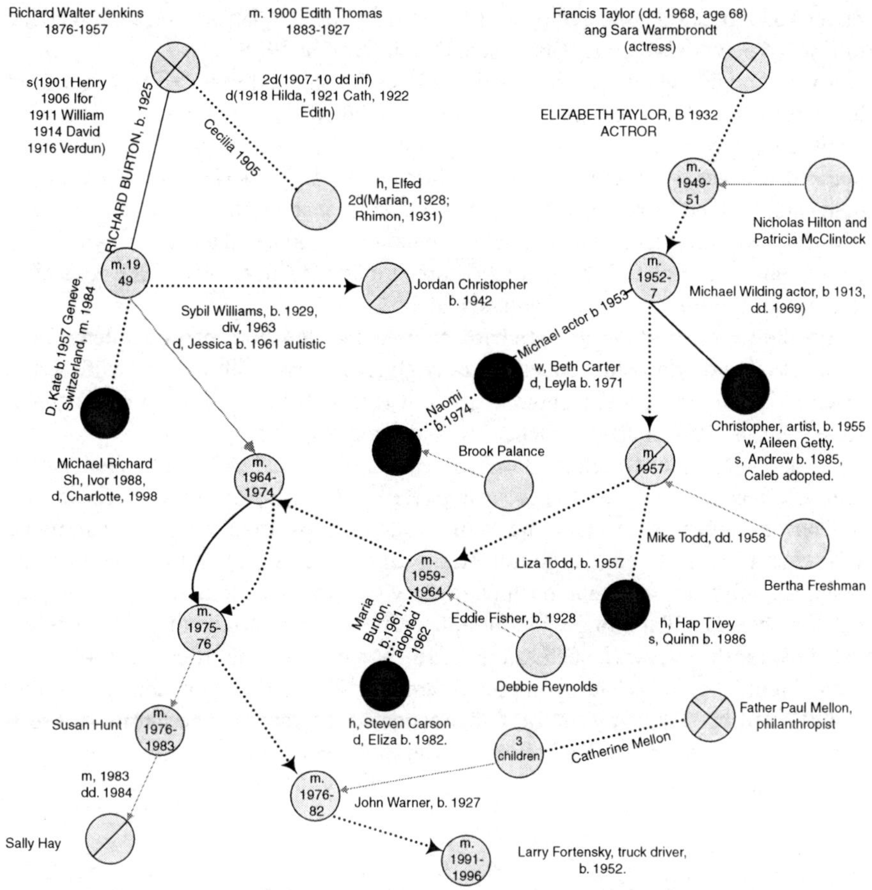

Fig. 9.4 Family history of Richard Burton and Elizabeth Taylor. *b* born, *d* daughter, *dd.* died, *h* husband, *m* marriage, *s* son, *w* wife

Figure 9.4 depicts Richard Burton's and Elizabeth Taylor's cumulative relations for each of their marital histories. Richard Burton was the tenth of eleven surviving children of Richard Walter Jenkins and Edith Thomas (Munn 2008). After his mother died when he was two years old, his sister Cecilia raised him with her children Marian and Rhimon. Richard's sister, like his parents, remained married to the same partner for life. Richard, however, departed from strict monogamy.

Richard's marriage to Sybil Williams in 1949 ended in divorce in 1963. They had two daughters, Jessica and Kate. Sybil remarried Jordan Christopher and Richard remarried Elizabeth Taylor, who brought to the marriage her three-year-old adopted daughter, Maria (Heymann 1995; Walker 1997). Maria was adopted in 1962 by Elizabeth and her fourth husband Eddie Fisher, whom she married after her third husband Mike Todd died in 1958, just one year after they married. Elizabeth also brought into the marriage her daughter Liza, who was one-year old at the time her father Todd died. As indicated by a filled circle in Fig. 9.4, Liza is currently married to Hap Tivey with whom she has a son, Quinn, born in 1986.

Even though Liza was Mike Todd's only child, she had two half brothers from her mother's earlier marriages. Her mother, Elizabeth, married Nicholas Hilton in 1949. They divorced in 1951 without any children. One year after divorce Elizabeth married her second husband, an actor, Michel Wilding. During thirteen years of marriage, they had two sons, Michael and Christopher. Both of them married and had children. Naomi, one of Michael's two daughters, married a previously married Brook Palance. Michael's brother Christopher married Aileen Getty. She gave birth to their son Andrew, and they adopted Caleb.

By the time Elizabeth and Richard married in 1964 both had completed their procreation and adoptions. Richard's only children were with his first wife Sybil. One of his daughters, Jessica born in 1961, was an autistic child. His first daughter, Kate born in 1957, married Michael Richard and had two children: son Ivor born 1968, and a daughter Charlotte born ten years later in 1978. All of Elizabeth's children also married and seem to have stable relationships. Nevertheless, because their mother had multiple partners, the family relationships are similar to those found in ancient Hawaii. Even though toward the end of the Hawaiian monarchy no one practiced polygamy, the relationships in early generations cumulated into complex kinship networks. Parenting with multiple partners today also results in a complex, extended kinship network such as that of Elizabeth Taylor and Richard Burton.

Serial monogamy creates compound families. The following example is further complicated by polygamy on the father's side of the family. The family of President Barack Hussein Obama includes serial monogamy and polygamy within one generation.

Geography and History of President Barack Obama's Family

The affinology chart of President Barack Obama's family culminates with the birth of his two daughters Malia and Natasha (Fig. 9.5). They inherited their mother's, Michelle LaVaughn Robinson, Southern origin. LaVaughn was the first name of her father's mother, a naming tradition used to affirm the importance of relationships and connections to the family ancestors (Mundy 2008, p. 2). Michelle Obama's parents emphasized education and self-discipline. She graduated from Princeton University and Harvard Law School (Lightfoot 2009).

Figure 9.5 shows President Obama's cultural, geographic, and genetic heritage. Even though both he and his wife are considered "African American," it is unlikely that their family roots would lead to a common origin within recorded history. President Obama's family history over the last three hundred years spans four continents: North America, Western Europe, Africa, and, through his relationship with his step-father, Asia (Obama 2004). Ethnic diversity in President Obama's background is truly remarkable. Through his mother's side of the family, his roots

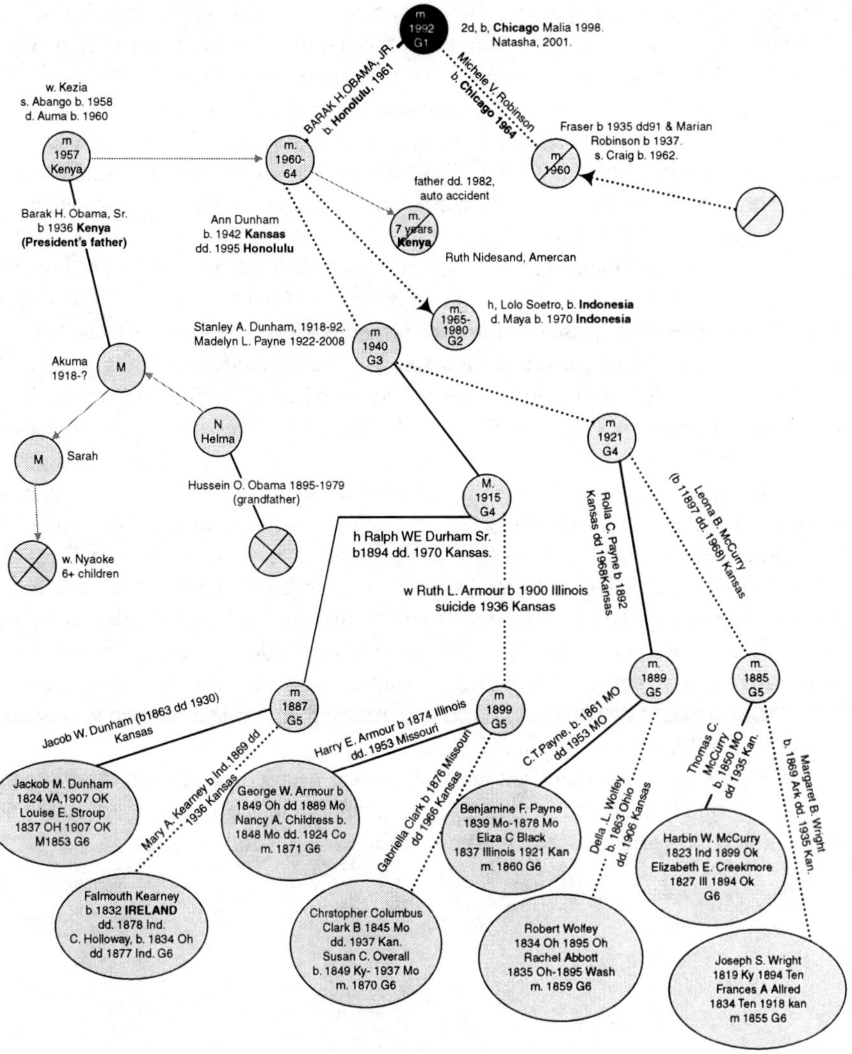

Fig. 9.5 Euro-African origins of President Barack H. Obama

are firmly established in the heartland of the United States and before that in Ireland (Reitwiesner 2010).

President Obama claims Irish heritage through his great, great, great grandmother Mary A. Kearney. Mary A. Kearney was a daughter of Falmouth Kearney, an immigrant born in Ireland in 1832. He died in Indiana in 1878. Mary's mother, C. Holloway, was born in Ohio in 1834. She died in Indiana in 1877. Mary Kearney married Jacob W. Dunham in 1887. Their son Ralph W.E. Durham married Ruth Armour who moved to Kansas from Illinois. She married at fifteen and at age thirty six she committed suicide. Their son Stanley A. Dunham married Madelyn L. Payne. They had a daughter Ann, their only child. Ann Durham married Barak Obama Sr. With the exception of one Irish immigrant in President Obama's family, four consecutive generations of ancestors on his mother's side of the family were born within seven contiguous states in the central region of the United States. These states were Illinois, Indiana, Kansas, Kentucky, Ohio, Oklahoma, and Tennessee.

The president's mother, Ann, broke a long-standing family tradition when she married outside of her family's ethnic origin. No one in the family, since C. Holloway of Ohio married Falmouth Kearney born in Ireland, departed from regional or ethnic ties of the family of origin. Ann married out of her nationality, region, race, and religion. Her first husband, Barack Hussein Obama, Sr. was a Black Kenyan raised as a Muslim but considered himself an atheist (Andersen 2009, p. 23). He and Ann met in 1960 at the University of Hawaii where they both attended school. When they married in 1960, Barack already had a wife Kezia and two children in Kenya. Barack and Ann were married for four years before she obtained a divorce. The dotted arrow in Fig. 9.5 shows Ann's remarriage in 1965 to Lolo Soetro, an Indonesian. They lived in Indonesia where she gave birth to daughter Maya in 1970.

Solid arrows in Fig. 9.5 show the similarity between marital paths of President Obama's father and his grandfather, Onynago. Both his father and his grandfather had multiple wives. His father's third wife Ruth Nidesand was similar to Ann in that she was Caucasian, American, and followed an academic career. This marriage ended in a divorce, because Ruth did not want to share her husband with a previous wife, Kezia Aoko. After divorce, Barack Sr. married an African woman with whom he had one child, George Obama (Obama 2010).

President Obama's father died in 1982 in a car accident, and his mother died in 1995 of ovarian cancer. His mother lived long enough to see her son married but not long enough to see her progeny continue through Malia and Natasha.

Chapter 10
The Future of the Affinograph

Abstract The future of the affinograph depends on its usefulness for imaging diverse and dynamic family structures. Some useful applications of graphic imaging in teaching, research, and clinical practice suggested in this chapter include:

1. modernization of record keeping in child welfare services,
2. research on consequences of prohibition of same-gender marriages,
3. development of assessment techniques for use in counseling and marital therapy, and
4. curriculum development in family life education.

The affinograph will probably be welcomed by those who have sought to define the family "regardless of blood, legal ties, adoption or marriage" (Polikoff 2008, p. 33; Powell et al. 2010). Affinographs represent such an expanded view of families as evidenced in the definition of the family used in this book:

> A family is a changing network of three or more relationships accumulated through descent and affinal unions such as marriage, civil unions, or informal unions, with an opportunity or an expectation to procreate, adopt, and raise children.

The affinograph definition of the family presumes that each person is an expert on his or her own family. Considering that families so defined tend to be complex, diverse, and dynamic there is a reason to suspect that the affinograph method for family imaging may have applications in teaching, research, and service across disciplines. Research on affinographs in social work is probably the most urgent. Institutions dealing with family problems and child welfare may find that record keeping with the aid of affinographs could be more efficient.

Affinographs may be used in counseling and family therapy. These professions have a long history of relying on genograms for mapping family constellations. Those who found genograms useful could also explore affinographs. For those who combine research with teaching, the affinographs may serve both purposes.

D. Jedlicka, *Affinographs*, DOI 10.1007/978-1-4419-9395-3_10,

Using Affinographs to Track Children and Their Families

Family service agencies tend to treat families according to the content of official forms and protocols used at intake. Protocols tend to define families without regard for a client's perception of "Who is the family?" Consequently, child services may omit the relevant family members. It is well known that fathers, no matter how attached to their children, are routinely omitted from the official definitions of the family. Similarly, other significant others remain unknown and unutilized.

The affinographs may have a promising future if social work agencies develop computer models for tracking children. An affinograph can serve as an algorithm between a graphic program and a data management program. Such computer applications could improve the tracking of children even when their parents change the residence. At this point, we can speculate that agencies entrusted with the care of children at risk would lose fewer children if their records were easily accessible, relevant, and inclusive. However, research is needed to substantiate or refute this contention.

Research on the Consequences of Prohibition of Same-Gender Marriages

Affinograph images of intervening relationships may serve as a theoretical framework for collecting evidence on the consequences of the ban of the same-gender marriages. Both sides of this argument consider their position to be "moral." Those opposed to the same-gender marriage argue that such a practice would weaken marriages in general. If their conclusion is correct, then prohibition could be justified. If they are not correct, would they be as likely to deny the right for the same-gender couples to marry?

Harris (2010) in his book, *The Moral Landscape: How Science Can Determine Human Values,* urges social scientists to use the scientific method to research moral issues. If research demonstrates that a social policy causes more harm than good, such a policy could be changed. The affinograph models postulate that divorce rates may be higher due to the mismatched sexual orientation in marriage. These intervening relationships could be responsible for involving more children in divorces than if there were no ban on the same-gender marriage. The affinograph could provide theoretical patterns of marital histories to estimate the number of children involved in divorces due to mismatched gender orientations.

Affinographs in Counseling and Marital Therapy

The distinction between marital therapy and counseling becomes blurred when a client's problem stems from family relationships. A counselor or a family therapist can use an affinograph to assess whether or not family issues are a problem.

Because affinographs are new, there are no published findings to confirm their clinical usefulness. Research on genograms, referenced elsewhere in this book, shows that images of family structures have been useful in clinical assessment. Because affinographs are also an imaging method, one could conjecture that the affinographs could be as useful for imaging dynamic families as the genograms have been in imaging static families.

An advantage of assessment with an affinograph is that its symbols can be standardized across disciplines. Because the affinograph symbols follow the graph theory, arbitrary deviation in practice may be unlikely. Any attempts to improve affinograph applications would conform to the mathematical axioms of the graph theory or else it would no longer be an affinograph. The grounding in the graph theory assures the consistency of applications and interpretations. Simultaneously, the affinograph assumptions minimize the "expert" bias. The client is treated as an expert on one's own relationships. Whether these relationships are ambiguous or clear, there is an affinograph symbol for each. If standardization of clinical technique is a goal, then the affinograph may have a future in clinical assessment and interventions.

Affinographs in Family Life Education

If the affinograph meets the desired pedagogical outcomes, it may become a standard method for teaching family life education. The affinograph method of graphic imaging is suited for illustrating changes in the family life cycle. This heuristic advantage may encourage educators to introduce affinographs through textbooks, lectures, and online teaching.

Regardless of the medium used, the affinograph could bring more clarity, accuracy, and precision in presenting family concepts to students. Definitions of even rudimentary concepts such as *family, family system, family structure*, and *family types* vary widely from textbook to textbook. While there is no agreement on what any of these concepts mean, everyone agrees that these concepts tend to be ambiguous. Having a clear definition and a method of representing a family as a dynamic system from a point of view of a person allows a teacher to assess the accuracy and precision of family concepts.

An image may be clear and accurate but not precise. For example, an image of a "single-parent family" may accurately represent an institutional conceptualization of a *family*. That representation, however, may not be precise. Where is the other parent? Where are uncles, aunts, and grandparents? Such inquiries increase precision and lead to the discussion of relevancy of broader family relationships.

Teaching about family systems requires a pedagogy free of politics, culture, and personal biases. The affinograph may promote such pedagogy. Affinograph images reveal a variety of families collectively referred to as "compound families." Compound families tend to occupy several households, share characteristics of polygamy, and represent cumulative, interlocking relationships. The affinograph images of such families tend to be clear, accurate, and precise.

Family life educators may also choose to use affinographs to introduce gender orientation issues into the family education curriculum. The way these issues are taught today may be handicapped by ideology. Pedagogical ideologies today accept as moral and ethical for one group of people to define marriage and family for another (Powell et al. 2010). The affinograph applications avoid ideology by empowering each individual to define the structure and the meaning of one's own family.

In short, the future of the affinograph depends on its usefulness. In an optimistic scenario, the affinograph may guide research, increase relevancy of clinical assessment, improve efficiency in child services, and enhance family life education.

References

Aldous, J., & Straus, M. A. (1966). Social networks and conjugal roles: A test of Bott's hypothesis. *Social Forces, 44,* 576–580.

Allen, E. S., Baucum, D. H., Burnett, C. K., Epstein, N. E., & Rankin-Esquer, L. A. (2001). Decision-making power, autonomy, and communication in remarried spouses compared with first-married spouses. *Family Relations, 50*(4), 326–334.

Allen, E. S., & Rhoades, G. K. (2008). Not all affairs are created equal: Emotional involvement with an extradyadic partner. *Journal of Sex & Marital Therapy, 34,* 51–65.

Allen, H. G. (1982). *The betrayal of Liliuokalani, last Queen of Hawaii, 1838–1917*. Honolulu: Mutual Publishing.

Allen, K. R., Blieszner, R., & Roberto, K. A. (2000). Families in the middle and later years: A review and critique of research in the 1990s. *Journal of Marriage and the Family, 62*(4), 911–926.

Amato, P. A. (2000). The consequences of divorce for adults and children. *Journal of Marriage and the Family, 62*(4), 1269–1287.

Andersen, C. (2009). *Barck and Michelle: Portrait of an American marriage*. New York: William Morrow.

Anderson, E. A., Kohler, J. K., & Letiecq, B. L. (2002). Low-income fathers and "Responsible Fatherhood" programs: A qualitative investigation of participants' experiences. *Family Relations, 51*(2), 148–155.

Apostel, L. (1961). Towards the formal study of models in the non-formal sciences. In H. Freudenthal (Ed.), *The concept of the role of the model in mathematics and natural and social sciences* (pp. 1–37). New York: Gordon & Breach.

Armesto, J. C. (2002). Developmental and contextual factors that influence gay fathers' Parental competence: A review of the literature. *Psychology of Men and Masculinity,* 3(2), 67–78.

Auger, J. R. (1976). *Behavioral systems and nursing*. Englewood Cliffs: Prentice Hall.

Barret, R. L., & Robinson, B. E. (1990). *Gay fathers*. Lexington: Lexington Books.

Barth, R. P., Greeson, J. K. P., Guo, S., Green, R. L., Hurley, S., & Sisson, J. (2007). Changes in family functioning and child behavior following intensive in-home therapy. *Child and Youth Services Review, 29,* 988–1009.

Becvar, D. S., & Becvar, R. J. (2000). *Family therapy: A systemic integration*. Boston: Allyn and Bacon.

Beer, W. R. (1989). *Strangers in the house: The world of stepsiblings and half-siblings*. New Brunswick: Transactions.

Bengtson, V. L. (2001). The Burgess award lecture: Beyond the nuclear family: The increasing importance of multigenerational bonds. *Journal of Marriage and the Family, 63*(1), 1–16.

Bernard, J. (1956). *Remarriage: A study of marriage*. New York: Dryden Press.

Bernstein, B. E., & Hartsell, T. (2000). *The portable ethicist for mental health professionals*. New York: Wiley.

D. Jedlicka, *Affinographs,* DOI 10.1007/978-1-4419-9395-3,

Block, J. (2009). *Open: Love, sex and life in an open marriage*. Berkeley: Seal Press.
Bos, H. M. W., Van Balen, F., & Van Den Boom, D. C. (2004). Experience of parenthood, couple relationship, social support, and child-rearing goals in planned lesbian mother families. *Journal of Child Psychology and Psychiatry, 45*(4), 755–764.
Bos, H. M. W., Gartell, N. K., Van Balen, F., Peyser, H., & Sanford, T. G. M. (2008). Children in planned lesbian families: A cross-cultural comparison between the United States and the Netherlands. *American Journal of Orthopsychiatry, 78*(2), 211–219.
Boteach, S. (2002). *Kosher adultery: Seduce and sin with your spouse*. Avon: Adams Media.
Bott, E. (1957). *Family and social network*. New York: Free Press.
Bowen, M. (1978). *Family therapy in clinical practice*. New York: Jason Aronson.
Bradt, J. (1980). *The family diagram*. Washington, DC: Groome Center.
Bragg, M. (1988). *Richard Burton: A life*. Boston: Little, Brown.
Bringle, R. G., & Buunk, B. P. (1991). Extradyadic relationships and sexual jealousy. In K. McKinney & S. Sprecher (Eds.), *Sexuality in close relationships* (pp. 135–153). Hillsdale: Erlbaum.
Broderick, C. B. (1972). Beyond the five conceptual frameworks: A decade of development in family theory. In C. B. Broderick (Ed.), *A decade of family research and action* (pp. 3–24). Minneapolis: National Council on Family Relations.
Bronson, P. (2005). Definitions of family. http://www.pobronson.com/factbook/pages/39.html. Accessed June 2010.
Broom, L., & Selznick, P. (1968). *Sociology: A text with adopted readings*. New York: Harper & Row.
Brown, E. M. (1999). *Affairs: A guide to working through the repercussions of infidelity*. San Francisco: Jossey-Bass.
Bunting, L., & McAuley, C. (2004). Research review: Teenage pregnancy and parenthood: The role of fathers. *Child and Family Social Work, 9*, 295–303.
Buric, O., & Zecevic, A. (1967, May). Family authority, marital satisfaction, and the social network in Yugoslavia. *Journal of Marriage and the Family, 29*, 325–336.
Busacker, G., & Saaty, T. L. (1965). *Finite graphs and networks: An introduction with applications*. New York: McGraw-Hill.
Butler, J. F. (2008). The family diagram and genogram: Comparison and contrasts. *The American Journal of Family Therapy, 36*, 169–180.
Cabrera, N., & Peters, H. E. (2000). Public policies and father involvement. *Marriage & Family Review, 29*(4), 295–315.
Cahill, S. (2004). *Same-sex marriage in the United States*. Lanham: Lexington Books.
Cancian, M., & Meyer, D. R. (2004). Fathers of children receiving welfare: Can they provide more child support? *Social Service Review, 78*(2), 179–206.
Carmody, D. C. (2000). Family abductions: An examination of the role of offender gender. *Gender Issues, 18*(2), 58–73.
Carstens, C. A. (2001). Defining the boundaries: Social worker assessment of sexual abuse in a cultural context—multivariate analysis of personal and professional factors influencing social workers' labeling of intimacy behavior. *Child and Family Social Work, 6*, 315–325.
Carvalho, M. J., Faustino, I., Nascimento, A., & Sales, C. M. D. (2008, September). Understanding Pamina's recovery: An application of the hermeneutic single-case design. *Counseling and Psychotherapy Research, 8*(3), 166–173.
Center for Disease Control and Prevention. (2008, December). *Sexually transmitted disease surveillance 2007*. Atlanta: Department of Health and Human Services.
Chambers, D. L. (1996). What if? The legal consequences of marriage and the legal needs of lesbian and gay male couples. *Michigan Law Review, 95*(2), 447–491.
Chang, J. (1999). Scripting extramarital affairs: Marital mores, gender politics, and infidelity in Taiwan. *Modern China, 25*(1), 69–99.
Chase, S. K. (2004). *Clinical judgment and communication in nurse practitioner practice*. Philadelphia: F. A. Davis Company.
Cherlin, A. J. (2004). The deinstitutionalization of American marriage. *Journal of Marriage and Family, 66*, 848–861.

Cherlin, A. J. (2005). American marriage in the early twenty-first century. *The Future of Children, 15*(2), 33–55.
Cherlin, A. J. (2010). *Public & private families*. New York: McGraw Hill.
Christopher, F. S., & Sprecher, S. (2000). Dating and other relationships: A decade review. *Journal of Marriage and Family, 62*(4), 999–1017.
Cluines, D. M., & Green, G. D. (1993). *Lesbian couples*. Seattle: Seal Press.
Coco, E. L., & Courtney, L. J. (2003). A family systems approach for preventing adolescent runaway behavior. *Family Therapy, 30*(1), 39–50.
Cohn, C. S., Mulroy, E., Tull, T., White, C., & Crowley, S. (2004). Housing plus services: Supporting vulnerable families in permanent housing. *Child Welfare, 83*(5), 509–527.
Coleman, M., Ganong, L. H., & Fine, M. (2000). Reinvestigating remarriage: Another decade of progress. *Journal of Marriage and the Family, 62*(4), 1288–1307.
Congress, E. P. (1994). The use of culture grams to assess and empower culturally diverse families. *Families in Society-The Journal of Contemporary Human Services, 75*(9), 531–540.
Cooley, C. (2000). The role of friends, in-laws, and other kin in father-perpetrated child physical abuse. *Child Welfare, 79*(4), 373–402.
Coohey, C., & Zhang, Y. (2006). The role of men in chronic supervisory neglect. *Child Maltreatment, 11*(1), 27–33.
Cooper, A. (1998). Sexuality and the internet: Surfing the way into the new millennium. *CyberPsychology and Behavior, 1*(2), 24–28.
Corey, G., & Callanan, P. (1993). *Issues and ethics in the helping professions*. Pacific Grove: Brook/Cole.
Cottrell, J., & Cashin, F. (1971). *Richard Burton very close up*. Englewood Cliffs: Prentice-Hall.
Crosbie-Burnett, M., & McClintic, K. M. (2000). Remarriage and recoupling: A stress perspective. In P. C. McKenry & S. J. Price (Eds.), *Families and change: Coping with stressful events and transitions*. Thousand Oaks: Sage.
Curran, L. (2003). Social work and fathers: Child support and fathering programs. *Social Work, 48*(2), 219–227.
Dansereau, D. F., Dees, S. M., & Simpson, D. D. (1994). Cognitive modularity: Implications for counseling and the representation of personal issues. *Journal of Counseling Psychology, 41*(4), 513–523.
Daughhetee, C. (2001, Spring). Using genograms as a tool for insight in college counseling. *Journal of College Counseling, 4*, 73–76.
Davenport, C. B. (1911/1972). *Heredity in relation to eugenics*. New York: Arno Press.
Davis, L., Geikie, G., & Schamess, G. (1988). The use of genograms in a group for latency age children. *International Journal of Group Psychotherapy, 38*(1), 189–210.
DeGeneva, M. K., & Rice, F. P. (2002). *Intimate relationships, marriages, & families*. Boston: McGraw Hill.
De Graaf, P. M., & Kalmijin, M. (2003). Alternative routes in the remarriage market: Competing-risk analysis of union formation after divorce. *Social Forces, 81*(4), 1459–1498.
DeMaria, R., Weeks, G., & Hof, L. (1999). *Focused genograms: Intergenerational assessment of individuals, couples, and families*. Philadelphia: Brunner/Mazel.
DeMaris, A. (2009). Distal and proximal influences on the risk of extramarital sex: A prospective study of longer duration marriages. *Journal of Sex Research, 46*(6), 597–607.
Denham, S. A. (2003). *Family health: A framework for nursing*. Philadelphia: F. A. Davis.
Devor, A. H. (2009). What are "we"? Where sexual orientation meets gender identity. In A. L. Ferber, K. Holcomb, & T. Wentling (Eds.), *Sex, gender, and sexuality: The new basics* (pp. 527–536). New York: Oxford University Press.
Dinerman, M. (2004). Definitions and their consequences. *Affilia: Journal of Women & and Social Work, 19*(4), 353, p5.
Duba, J. D., Graham, M. A., Britzman, M., & Minatrea, N. (2009). Introducing the "basic need genogram" in reality therapy-based marriage and family counseling. *International Journal of Reality Therapy, 28*(2), 15–19.
Duberman, L. (1977). *Marriage and other alternatives*. New York: Praeger.

Dudley, J. R. (2007). Helping nonresidential fathers: The case for teen and adult unmarried fathers. *Families in Society, 88*(2), 171–181.
Durbin, J. (2003). Married man, bored, seeks sex kitten. *Maclean's, 116*(40), 20.
Earls, F., & Carlson, M. (2001). The social ecology of child health and well-being. *Annual Review of Public Health, 22,* 143–146.
Eichholz, A. (2003). Managing cutoff through family research. In P. Titelman (Ed.), *Emotional cutoff: Bowen family systems theory Perspectives* (pp. 173–196). New York: Haworth Clinical Practice Press.
Einstein, E. (1982). *The stepfamily: Living, loving and learning.* New York: Macmillan.
Elmslie, B., & Tebaldi, E. (2008). So, what did you do last night? The economics of infidelity. *Kyklos, 61*(3), 391–410.
Eskridge, W. N., Jr. (1993). A history of same-sex marriage. *Virginia Law Review, 79*(7), 1419–1513.
Fagan, J., Bernd, E., & Whiteman, V. (2007). Adolescent fathers' parenting stress, social support, and involvement with infants. *Journal of Research on Adolescence, 17*(1), 1–22.
Falke, S., & Larson, J. (2007). Premarital predictors of remarital quality: Implications for clinicians. *Contemporary Family Therapy: An International Journal, 29*(1/2), 9–23.
Farber, B. (1964). *Family: Organization and interaction.* San Francisco: Chandler Publishing.
Farber, B. (1981). *Conceptions of kinship.* New York: Elsevier.
Featherstone, B. (2004). Fathers matter: A research review. *Children & Society, 18*(4), 312–319.
Feinberg, J., & Bakeman, R. (1994). Sexual orientation and three generational family: Patterns in a clinical sample of heterosexual and homosexual men. *Journal of Gay and Lesbian Psychotherapy, 2*(2), 65–76.
Fields, J. (2003, June). *Children's living arrangements and characteristics: March 2002.* Current Population Reports, P20–547. U. S. Census Bureau.
Fields, J., & Casper, L. M. (2001). *America's families and living arrangements.* Current Population Reports, P20–537. U. S. Census Bureau.
Fisher, S., & Greenberg, R. P. (1996). *Freud scientifically reappraised: Testing the theories and therapy.* New York: Wiley.
Flanagan, C. (2009). Why marriage matters? *Time, 174*(1), 45–49.
Foster, B. L., & Seidman, S. B. (1992). A formal unification of anthropological kinship and social network methods. In L. C. Freeman, D. R. White, & A. K. Romney (Eds.), *Research methods in social network analysis.* New Brunswick: Transaction Publishers.
Freeman, E. M., & Couchonnal, G. (2006). Narrative and culturally based approaches in practice with families. *Families in Society, 87*(2), 198–208.
Freeman, L. C. (2000). Visualizing social networks. *Journal of Social Structure, 1*(1): 4. http://www.cmu.edu/joss/content/articles/volume1/Freeman.html. Accessed August 2007.
Freeman, L. C. (2004). *The development of social network analysis: A study in sociology of science.* Vancouver: Empirical Press.
Friedman, S., & Forsyth, S. (1994). *Secret loves: Women with two lives.* New York: Crown.
Gameiro, S., Boivin, J., Canavarro, M. C., Moura-Ramos, M., & Soares, I. (2010). Social nesting: Changes in social network and support across the transition to parenthood in couples that conceived spontaneously or through assisted reproductive techniques. *Journal of Family Psychology, 24*(2), 175–187.
Ganong, L. H., & Coleman, M. (1989). Preparing for remarriage: Anticipating the issues, seeking solutions. *Family Relations, 38*(1), 28–33.
Garrett, A. (1982). *Interviewing: Its principles and methods* (3rd ed.). Milwaukee: Family Service America.
Gee, C. B., & Rhodes, J. E. (2003). Adolescent mothers' relationship with their children's biological fathers: Social support, social strain, and relationship continuity. *Journal of Family Psychology, 17*(3), 370–383.
Geher, G. (2000). Perceived and actual characteristics of parents and partners: A test of Freudian model of mate selection. *Current Psychology, 19*(3), 194–214.
Gertler, S., & Lopez, A. (2005). *To love, honor, and betray.* New York: Hyperion.

Gibbons, J., Conroy, S., Bell, C., & Gordon D. (1995). *Development after physical abuse in early childhood: A follow up study of children on child protection register*. London: HMSO.

Glass, S. P., & Wright, T. L. (1992). Justifications for extramarital relationships: The association between attitudes, behaviors, and gender. *The Journal of Sex Research, 29*(3), 361–387.

Glick, P. C. (1977). Updating the life cycle of the family. *Journal of Marriage and the Family, 39*(1), 5–14.

Goddard, H. H. (1912). *The Kallikak family*. New York: Macmillan.

Goldenberg, I., & Goldenberg, H. (2008). *Family therapy: An overview*. Pacific Grove: Thomson-Brooks/Cole.

Grbich, C. (1999). *Qualitative research in health: An introduction*. Thousand Oaks: Sage.

Griffin, V. (1999). *The mistress: Histories, myths and interpretations of the 'other woman'*. New York: Bloomsbury.

Guerin, P. J., & Pendagast, E. G. (1976). Evaluation of family system and genorgram. In P. J. Guerin, Jr (Ed.), *Family therapy: Theory and practice* (pp. 450–464). New York: Gardner Press.

Guerin, P. J., Fogarty, T. F., Fay, L. F., & Kautto, J. G. (1996). *Working with relationship triangles: The one-two-three of psychotherapy*. New York: Guilford Press.

Guhl, E., & Koner, W. (1989). *Everyday life among the Greeks and Romans*. New York: Crescent Books.

Hansen, F. J., Fallon, A. E., & Novotny, S. (1991). The relationship between social network structure and marital satisfaction in distressed and nondistressed couples: A pilot study. *Family Therapy—The Journal of the California Graduate School of Family Psychology, 18*(2), 101–114.

Harary, F. (1972). *Graph theory*. Reading: Addison-Wesley.

Harary, F., & Batell, M. (1981). What is a system? *Social Networks, 3,* 29–40.

Harary, F., & White, D. R. (2001). P-systems: A structural model of kinship studies. *Connections, 24*(2), 35–46.

Harary, F., Norman, R. Z., & Cartwright, D. (1965). *Structural models*. New York: Wiley.

Hardy, K. V., & Laszloffy, T. A. (1995). The cultural genogram—Key to training culturally competent family therapists. *Journal of Marital and Family Therapy, 21*(3), 227–247.

Harris, S. (2010). *The moral landscape: How science can determine human values*. New York: Free Press.

Hawkins, J. (2007). My two dads: Challenging gender stereotypes in applying California's supreme court cases to gay couples. *Family Law Quarterly, 41*(3), 623–638.

Hein, H. (2000). *Sexual detours: Infidelity and intimacy at the crossroads*. New York: Saint Martin's Press.

Herzog, M. J., Umana-Taylor, A. J., Madden-Derdich, D. A., & Leonard, S. A. (2007). Adolescent mothers' perceptions of fathers' parental involvement: Satisfaction and desire for involvement. *Family Relations, 56*(3), 244–257.

Heymann, C. D. (1995). *Liz: An intimate biography of Elizabeth Taylor*. New York: Birch Lane Press.

Hobart, C. (1988). The family system in remarriage: An exploratory study. *Journal of Marriage and the Family, 50*(3), 469–661.

Hodge, D. R. (2001). Spiritual genograms: A generational approach to assessing spirituality. *Social Work, 46,* 203–214.

Hodge, D. R. (2005). Developing a spiritual assessment toolbox: A discussion of the strengths and limitations of five different assessment methods. *Health & Social Work, 30*(4), 314–323.

Hohengarten, W. M. (1994). Same-sex marriage and the right of privacy. *The Yale Law Journal, 103*(6), 1495–1531.

Holstein, J. A., & Gubrium, J. (1999). What is family? Further thoughts on a social constructionist approach. In B. H. Settles, S. K. Steinmetz, G. W. Peterson, & M. B. Sussman (Eds.), *Concepts and definitions of family for the 21st century*. New York: The Haworth Press.

Holzner, S. (2008). *Using Microsoft Office Visio 2007*. Indianapolis: Que.

Hook, J. L. (2006). Care in context: Men's unpaid work in 20 countries, 1965–2003. *American Sociological Review, 71,* 639–660.

Horn, W. F. (2006). Fatherhood, cohabitation and marriage. *Gender Issues, 23*(4), 22–35.

Howard, B. J., & Broughton, D. D. (2004). The pediatrician's role in the prevention of missing children. *Pediatrics, 114*(4), 1100–1105.

Howell, N. (1988). Understanding simple social structures: Kinship units and ties. In B. Wellman & S. D. Berkowitz (Eds.), *Social structures: A network approach*. New York: Cambridge University Press.

Hudson, H., Nutter, R. W., & Galaway, B. (1994). Treatment foster care programs: A review of evaluation research and suggested directions. *Social Work Research, 18,* 198–210.

Hughes, S. M., Harrison, M. A., & Gallup, G. G. (2004). Sex differences in mating strategies: Mate guarding, infidelity and multiple concurrent sex partners. *Sexualities, Evolution, and Gender, 6*(1), 3–13.

Hurd, G. E., Pattison, M., & Llamas, R. (1981). Models of social network intervention. *Family Therapy, 3*(1), 246–257.

Ingoldsby, B. B., & Smith, S. D. (2006). *Families in global and multicultural perspective*. Thousand Oaks: Sage.

Jankowiak, W., Nell, M. D., & Buckmaster, A. (2002). Managing infidelity: A cross-cultural perspective. *Ethnology, 41*(1), 85–101.

Jedlicka, D. (1975a). *Ethnic serial marriages in Hawaii: An application of a sequential preference model.* Dissertation, The University of Hawaii at Manoa.

Jedlicka, D. (1975b, December). Serial marriage networks: A study of change in the American family. Paper presented at the Social Networks Colloquium, Social Sciences and Linguistic Institute, The University of Hawaii, Honolulu.

Jedlicka, D. (1980). A test of the psychoanalytic theory of mate selection. *Journal of Social Psychology, 112,* 295–299.

Jedlicka, D. (1984). Indirect parental influence on mate selection: A test of the psychoanalytic theory. *Journal of Marriage and the Family, 46,* 65–70.

Jedlicka, D. (1985). Sex inequality in marriage and work as a consequence of age differences at marriage. In L. D. Knezek, M. C. Barrett, & S. K. Collins (Eds.), *Women and work.* The University of Texas at Arlington, Women and Work Research & Resource Center.

Jedlicka, D. (2000). The use of genographs in family assessment of serial monogamy. *Connections, 25*(1), 135.

Jenkins, D. (1993). *Richard Burton—A brother remembered.* London: Century.

Jensen, M. S. (1974). Role differentiation in female homosexual quasi-marital unions. *Journal of Marriage and the Family, 36*(2), 360–367.

Kadushin, A., & Kadushin, G. (1997). *The social work interview: A guide for human service professional.* New York: Columbia University Press.

Kahn, R. L., & Cannell, C. F. (1957). *The dynamics of interviewing: Theory, technique, and cases.* New York: Wiley.

Kando, T. M. (1978). *Sexual behavior and family life in transition.* New York: Elsevier.

Kappeler, V. E., & Potter, G. W. (2005). The myth and fear of missing children (Chap. 3., pp. 53–75). In *Mythology of crime and criminal justice.* Long Grove: Waveland Press.

Katz, J. (1985). *Gay, American history. Lesbians and gay men in the U.S.A.* New York: Harper & Row.

Keams, J. N., & Leonard, K. E. (2004). Social networks, structural interdependence, and marital quality over the transition to marriage: A prospective analysis. *Journal of Family Psychology, 18*(2), 383–395.

Kelly, B. J. (2003). Toward undoing cutoff: A twenty-five-year perspective. In P. Titelman (Ed.), *Emotional cutoff: Bowen family systems theory perspectives* (pp. 139–158). New York: Haworth Clinical Practice Press.

Kenney, C. (2004). Cohabiting couple, filing jointly? Resources pooling and U.S. poverty policies. *Family Relations, 53*(2), 237–247.

Kenyon, G. L., Chong, K., Enkoff-Sage, M., Hill, C., Mays, C., & Rochelle, L. (2003). Public adoption by gay and lesbian parents in North Carolina: Policy and practice. *Families in Society, 84*(4), 571–575.

Kephart, W., & Jedlicka, D. (1991). *Family, society and the individual.* New York: Harper Collins.

Kielty, S. (2005). Mothers are non-resident parents too: A consideration of mother's perspectives on non-residential parenthood. *Journal of Social Welfare and Family Law, 27*(1), 1–16.

Klovdahl, A. S. (1981). A note on images of networks. *Social Networks, 3,* 197–214.

Knoke, D., & Yang, S. (2008). *Social network analysis.* Los Angeles: Sage.

Kohler, J. K., Anderson, E. A., Oravecz, L., & Braun, B. (2004). Relationship constellations and dynamics of low-income rural mothers. *Affilia: Journal of Women & Social Work, 19*(2), 173–185.

Kramer, L. (1997). Same sex marriage, conflict of laws, and the unconstitutional public policy. *The Yale Law Journal, 106*(7), 1965–2008.

Kreider, R. M. (2005, February). *Number, timing and duration of marriages and divorces: 2001.* Current Population Reports, P70–97. U. S. Censuses Bureau.

Kreider, R. M., & Fields, J. (2002, February). *Number, timing and duration of marriages and divorces: 2001.* Current Population Reports, P70–80. U. S. Censuses Bureau.

Lamanna, M. A., & Riedmann, A. (2006). *Marriages & families: Making choices in a diverse society.* Belmont: Thomson Higher Education.

Lamb, M. E. (2004). *The role of the father in child's development.* Hoboken: Wiley.

Lansford, J. E., Ceballo, R., Abbey, A., & Stewart, A. J. (2001). Does family structure matter? A comparison of adoptive, two-parent biological, single-mother, stepfather, and stepmother households. *Journal of Marriage and the Family, 63*(3), 840–851.

Laumann, E. O., Gagnon, J. H., Michael, R. T., & Michaels, S. (1994). *The social organization of sexuality: Sexual practices in the United States.* Chicago: The University of Chicago Press.

Lawson, A. (1988). *Adultery: An analysis of love and betrayal.* New York: Basic Books.

Lazar, A., & Guttmann, J. (2005). Adolescents' perception of the ideal mate: Its relationship to parental characteristics intact and nonintact families. *Family Therapy, 32*(1), 31–38.

Levi-Strauss, C. (1949/1969). *The elementary structure of kinship.* Boston: Beacon Press.

Lewis, K. G. (1989). The use of color-coded genograms in family therapy. *Journal of Marital and Family Therapy, 15*(2), 169–176.

Li, Q., & Racine, J. (2004). Predictor relevance and extramarital affairs. *Journal of Applied Econometrics, 19*(4), 533–535.

Lightfoot, E. (2009). *Michelle Obama.* Guilford: Lyons Press.

Like, R. C., Rogers, J., & McGoldrick, M. (1988). Reading and interpreting genograms: A systemic approach. *The Journal of Family Practice, 26*(4), 407–412.

Liliuokalani, L. (2007). *Hawaii's story by Hawaii's Queen.* Honolulu: Mutual Publishing.

Lim, S., & Nakamoto, T. (2008). Genograms: Use in therapy with Asian families with diverse cultural heritages. *Contemporary Family Therapy, 30,* 199–219.

Lippa, R. A. (2007). The preferred traits of mates in a cross-national study of heterosexual and homosexual men and women: An examination of biological and cultural influences. *Archives of Sex Behavior, 36,* 193–208.

Loper, A. B., & Tuerk, E. H. (2006). Parenting programs for incarcerated parents. *Criminal Justice Policy Review, 17*(4), 407–427.

Macfarlane, A. (1883). Analysis of relationships of consanguinity and affinity. *Journal of the Royal Anthropological Institute of Great Britain and Ireland, 12,* 46–63.

Madhubuti, H. R. (1990). *Black men: Obsolete, single, dangerous? African American family in transition.* Chicago: Third World Press.

Maheu, M. M., & Subotnik, R. B. (2001). *Infidelity on the internet.* Naperville: Sourcebook.

Maluccio, A. N., Pine, B. A., & Tracy, E. M. (2002). *Social work practice with families and children.* New York: Columbia University Press.

Manning, W. D., & Smock, P. J. (2000). "Swapping" families: Serial parenting and economic support for children. *Journal of Marriage and the Family, 62*(1), 111–122.

Manning, W. D., Longmore, M. A., & Giordano, P. C. (2007, August). The changing institution of marriage: Adolescents' expectations to cohabit and to marry. *Journal of Marriage and Family, 69*, 559–575.

Maple, F. F. (1985). *Dynamic interviewing: An introduction to counseling*. Beverly Hills: Sage.

Marlin, E. (1989). *Genograms: The new tool for exploring the personality, career, and love patterns you inherit*. Chicago: Contemporary Books.

Marsiglo, W., & Day, R. D. (2000). Exploring fatherhood diversity: Implications for conceptualizing father involvement. *Marriage & Family Review, 29*(4), 269–294.

Mason, M. A. (2011). The modern American stepfamily. In S. J. Ferguson (Ed.), *Shifting the center: Understanding contemporary families*. New York: McGraw Hill.

Massey, R. F., Comey, S., & Just, R. L. (1988). Integrating genograms and script matrices. *Transactional Analysis Journal, 18*(4), 325–335.

Mathews, J. D., & Cramer, J. P. (2006). Envisioning the adoption process to strengthen gay- and lesbian-headed families: Recommendations for adoption professionals. *Child Welfare, 85*(2), 317–340.

Mattaini, M. A. (1997). Visualizing practice with children and families. In J. T. Pardeck & M. J. Markward (Eds.), *Reassessing social work: Practice with children*. Amsterdam: Gordon and Breach.

Maza, C. (2002a). Young dads: The effects of a parenting program on urban African-American adolescent fathers. *Adolescence, 37*(148), 681–693.

Maza, C. (2002b). And then the world fell apart. The children of incarcerated fathers. *Families in Society, 83*(5/6), 521–529.

McGill, D. W. (1992). The cultural story in multicultural family therapy. *Families in Society, 73*(6), 339–349.

McGinnis, T. (1981). *More than just a friend: The joys and disappointments of extramarital affairs*. Englewood Cliffs: Prentice-Hall.

McGoldrick, M., & Gerson, R. (1985). *Genograms in family assessment*. New York: W. W. Norton.

McGoldrick, M., Gerson, R., & Petry, S. (2008). *Genograms: Assessment and intervention* (3rd ed.). New York: W. W. Norton.

McGoldrick, M., Gerson, R., & Shellenberger, S. (1999). *Genograms: Assessment and intervention*. New York: W. W. Norton.

McKinnon, M., Davies, L., & Rains, P. (2001). Taking account of men in the lives of teenage mothers. *Affilia: Journal of Women & Social Work, 16*(1), 80–99.

McMillen, J. C., & Groze, V. (1994, July–August). Using placement genograms in child welfare practice. *Child Welfare, 73*(4), 307–318.

McRay, L., & Schwarz, T. (1990). *Kept women: Confessions from a life of luxury*. New York: William Morrow.

Mead, G. H. (1934). *Mind, self & society from the standpoint of a social behaviorist*. Chicago: The University of Chicago Press.

Meek, R. (2007). The parenting possible selves of young fathers in prison. *Psychology, Crime & Law, 13*(4), 371–382.

Meezan, W., & Rouch, J. (2005). Gay marriages, same-sex parenting, and America's children. *The Future of Children, 15*(2), 97–115.

Minkovitz, M. S. (1971). Social networks and innovations in the division of labor between men and women in the family and in the community: A study of Moroccan immigrants in Israel. *The Canadian Review of Sociology and Anthropology, 8*(4), 1–17.

Moats, D. (2007). Civil unions in Vermont: Public reason improvised. *Perspectives on Politics, 1*(1), 131–135.

Moehling, C. M. (2002). Broken homes: The "missing" children of the 1910 census. *Journal of Interdisciplinary History, 33*(2), 205–233.

Morgan, L. H. (1870/1997). *Systems of consanguinity and affinity of the human family*. Lincoln: University of Nebraska Press.

Morrison, D. R., & Ritualo, A. (2000). Routes to children's economic recovery after divorce: Are cohabitation and remarriage equivalent? *American Sociological Review, 65*(4), 560–580.

Mosher, W. D., Chandra, A., & Jones, J. (2005). *Sexual behavior and selected health measures: Men and women 15–44 years of age in the United States, 2002. Advance Data from Vital and Health Statistics, No. 363*. Hyattsville: National Center for Health Statistics.
Moss, B. (2003). Research into practice. *Community Care,* (1458), 47.
Mundy, L. (2008). *Michelle: A biography*. New York: Simon & Schuster.
Munn, M. (2008). *Richard Burton prince of players*. New York: Skyhorse Publishing.
Myers, M. L. (1990, June). Personal consequences of the sexually open marriage. *Dissertation Abstracts International, 50*(12-B, Pt. 1), 5927.
Naphy, W. (2002). Sodomy in early modern Geneva: Various definitions, diverse verdicts. In T. Betteridge (Ed.), *Sodomy in early modern Europe* (pp. 94–111). Manchester: Manchester University Press.
Nelson, L. (2005). Fathers and daughters: A needed course in family studies. *Marriage & Family Review, 38*(3), 1–13.
Nichols, M. P., & Schwartz, R. C. (2006). *The essential of family therapy* (3rd ed.). Boston: Pearson.
Noble, M. (1973). Social network: Its use as a conceptual framework in family analysis. In J. Boissevain & J. C. Mitchell (Eds.), *Network analysis: A study of human interaction* (pp. 3–14). Paris: Mouton.
Norton, A. J., & Glick, P. C. (1976). Marital instability: Past, present, and future. *Journal of Social Issues, 32*(10), 5–20.
Obama, B. (2004). *Dreams from my father*. New York: Three Rivers Press.
Obama, G. (2010). *Homeland: An extraordinary story of hope and survival*. New York: Simon & Schuster.
O'Neill, N., & O'Neill, G. (1972). *Open marriage: A new life style for couples*. New York: M. Evans.
Ore, O. (1960). Sex in graphs. *Proceedings of the American Mathematical Society, 11,* 533–539.
Paine, D. F. (2005). Evidence issues in a church triangle trial. *Tennessee Bar Journal, 41*(10), 22–23.
Parent, C., Saint-Jacques, M., Beaudry, M., & Robitaille, C. (2007). Stepfather involvement in social intervention made by youth protective services in stepfamilies. *Child & Family Social Work, 12*(3), 229–238.
Parke, R. D. (2004). Development in the family. *Annual Review of Psychology, 55,* 365–399.
Patterson, C. J. (2006). Children of lesbian and gay parents. *Current Directions in Psychological Science, 15*(5), 241–244.
Pattison, E. M. (1981). Introduction: The social network paradigm. *Family Therapy, 3*(4), 241–245.
Pattison, E. M., Llamas, R., & Hurd, G. E. (1979). Social network mediation of anxiety. *Psychiatric Annals, 9*(9), 56–67.
Peterson, G. W., & Steinmetz, S. K. (2000). The diversity of fatherhood: Change, constancy and contradiction. *Marriage & Family Review, 29*(4), 315–323.
Pippin, J. A. (1990). *Developing casework skills*. Newbury Park: Sage.
Polikoff, N. D. (1993). We will get what we ask for: Why legalizing gay and lesbian marriage will not "dismantle the legal structure of gender in every marriage." *Virginia Law Review, 79*(7), 1535–1550.
Polikoff, N. D. (2008). *Beyond (straight and gay) marriage: Valuing all families under the law*. Boston: Beacon Press.
Potter-Phillips, D. (1999, July–August). History of genealogy. *Family Chronicle*, http://www.family.chronicle.com/HistoryofGenealogy.html. Accessed May 2010.
Powell, B., Bolzendahl, C., Geist, C., & Steelman, L. C. (2010). *Counted out: Same sex relations and Americans' definitions of family*. New York: Sage.
Preston, S. H. (1975, May). Estimating the proportion of American marriages that end in divorce. *Sociological Methods & Research, 3,* 435–460.
Previti, D. (2004). Is infidelity a cause or a consequence of poor marital quality? *Journal of Social and Personal Relationships, 21*(2), 217–230.

Price, S. J., McKenry, P. C., & Murphy, M. J. (2000). *Family across time*. Los Angeles: Roxbury.
Proffitt, F. (2005, June). Infidelity has its benefits. *Science Now*, 4–5.
Rao, K., Bhaskaran, S. A., & Subbakrishna, D. K. (2001). Support utilization in the context of chronic strain. *Family Therapy—The Journal of the California Graduate School of Family Psychology, 28*(3), 143–156.
Reitman, D., Gross, A. M., & Messer, S. C. (1995). Role of family and home environment. In V. B. Van Haseelt & M. Hersen (Eds.), *Handbook of adolescent psychopathology a guide to diagnosis and treatment* (pp. 621–652). New York: Lexington Books.
Reitwiesner, W. A. (2010). Ancestry of Barack Obama. http://www.wargs.com/political/obama.html. Accessed 24 March 2010.
Rigazio-DiGilio, S. A., Ivey, A. E., Kunkler-Peck, K. P., & Grady, L. T. (2005). *Community genograms: Using individual, family and cultural narratives with clients*. New York: Teachers College, Columbia University.
Rivers, W. H. R. (1900). A genealogical method of collecting social and vital records. *Journal of the Anthropological Institute of Great Britain and Ireland, 30,* 74–82.
Rivers, W. H. R. (1910). The genealogical method of anthropological inquiry. *The Sociological Review, 3,* 1–12.
Roberto, L. G. (1992). *Transgenerational family therapies*. New York: Guilford Press.
Roggman, L. A., Boyce, L. K., Cook, G. A., & Cook, J. (2002). Getting dads involved: Fathers involvement with head start and with their children. *Infant Mental Health Journal, 23*(1/2), 62–78.
Roser-Strier, D. (2001). Reducing risk for children in changing cultural contexts: Recommendations for intervention and training. *Child Abuse and Neglect, 25*(2), 231–248.
Rowse, A. L. (1997). *Homosexual in history*. New York: Carroll & Graf.
Ruggles, S., & Brower, S. (2003). Measurement of household and family composition in the United States, 1850–2000. *Population and Development Review, 29*(1), 73–101.
Sadler, J. D. (1988). *Families in transition: An annotated bibliography*. Hamden: Archon Books.
Saleh, M. F., Buzi, R. S., Weinman, M. L., & Smith, P. B. (2005). The nature of connections: Young fathers and their children. *Adolescence, 40*(159), 513–523.
Salloway, J. C., & Dillon, P. B. (1973). A comparison of family networks and friend networks in health care utilization. *The Journal of Comparative Family Studies, 4*(1), 131–142.
Scheinkman, M. (2005, June). Beyond the trauma of betrayal: Reconsidering affairs in couple therapy. *Family Process, 44*(2), 227–244.
Schmitt, D. P. (2004). The big five related to risky sexual behavior across 10 world regions: Differential personality associations of sexual promixcuity and relationship infidelity. *European Journal of Personality, 18*(4), 301–319.
Scourfield, J. (2006). The challenge of engaging fathers in the child protection process. *Critical Social Policy, 26*(2), 440–449.
Segrin, C., & Flora, J. (2005). *Family communication*. Mahwah: Erlbaum.
Settles, B. H. (1999). Definitions of the family: Professional and personal issues. In B. H. Settles, S. K. Steinmetz, G. W. Peterson, & M. B. Sussman (Eds.), *Concepts and definitions of family for the 21st century*. New York: Haworth Press.
Settles, B. H., Steinmetz, S. K., Peterson, G. W., & Sussman, M. B. (1999). *Concepts and definitions of family for the 21st century*. New York: Haworth Press.
Sheafor, B. W., Horejsi, C. R., & Horejsi, G. A. (2007). *Techniques and guidelines for social work practice*. Boston: Allyn and Bacon.
Shellenberger, S., Dent, M. M., Davis-Smith, M., Seale, J. P., Weintraut, R., & Wright, T. (2007). Cultural genogram: A tool for teaching and practice. *Families, Systems, & Health, 25*(4), 367–381.
Simon, D., & Burns, E. (1997). *The corner: A year in life of an inner city neighborhood*. New York: Broadway Books.
Skolnick, A. S., & Skolnick, J. H. (2007). *Family in transition*. New York: Longman.
Sluzki, C. E. (2010). Personal social networks and health: Conceptual and clinical implications of their reciprocal impact. *Families, Systems & Health, 28*(1), 1–18.

Smith, D. S. (2005). *Understanding infidelity: Why more wives are unfaithful*. Avon: Adams Media.

Smock, P. J., & Manning, W. (2010). New couples, new families: The cohabitation revolution in the United States. In B. J. Risman (Ed.), *Families as they really are* (pp. 131–139). New York: W. W. Norton.

Snider, M. (1992). *Process family therapy: An eclectic approach to family therapy*. Boston: Allyn and Bacon.

Sprenkle, D. H., & Fisher, B. L. (1978). Family therapy conceptualization and use of "case notes." *Family Therapy, 5*(2), 177–183.

Staheli, L. (1997). *Triangles: Understanding, preventing and surviving affairs*. New York: Haper-Collins.

Starbuck, G. H. (2010). *Families in context*. Boulder: Paradigm.

Steiner, H. (2004). *Handbook of mental health interventions in children and adolescents*. San Francisco: Jossey-Bass.

Strah, D. (2003). *Gay dads: A celebration of fatherhood*. New York: Jeremy P. Tucker/Putnam.

Strong, B., DeVault, C., Sayad, B. W., & Cohen, T. F. (2001). *The marriage and family experience*. Belmont: Wadsworth/Thompson Learning.

Strug, D., & Wilmore-Schaeffer, R. (2003). Fathers in the social work literature: Policy and practice implications. *Families in Society, 84*(4), 503–511.

Summers, J. A., Boller, K., & Raikes, H. (2004). Preferences and perceptions about getting support expressed by low-income fathers. *Fathers, 2*(1), 61–82.

Summers, J. A., Boller, K., Schiffman, R. F., & Raikes, H. H., (2006). The meaning of "good fatherhood": Low-income fathers' social construction of their roles. *Parenting Science and Practice, 6*(2), 145–165.

Swainson, M., & Tasker, F. (2006). Genograms redrewn: Lesbian couples define their families. In J. J. Bigner (Ed.), *An introduction to GLBT family studies* (pp. 89–115). New York: Haworth Press.

Talmon, M. (1990). *Single session therapy*. San Francisco: Jossey-Bass.

Talmon, M. (1993). *Single session solutions*. Reading: Addison-Wesley.

Taub, A. (2007). Fit or unfit? Homosexuality and parenting. *The Journal of Contemporary Legal Issues, 16*(29), 29–33.

Taylor, H. F. (1970). *Balance in small groups*. New York: Van Nostrand Reinhold.

Taylor, R. (1997). *Love affairs: Marriages & infidelity*. Amherst: Prometheus Books.

Teachman, D. J., Tedrow, L. M., & Crowder, K. D. (2000). The changing demography of America's families. *Journal of Marriage and the Family, 62*(4), 1234–1246.

Thoburn, J., & Whitman, D. M. (2004). Clergy affairs: Emotional investment, longevity of relationships and affair partners. *Pastoral Psychology, 52*(6), 491–506.

Thomas, A. J. (1998). Understanding culture and worldview in family systems: Use of the multicultural genogram. *The Family Journal, 6*(1), 24–32.

Titelman, P. (2003). *Emotional cutoff: Bowen family systems theory perspective*. New York: Haworth Clinical Practice Press.

Tjon Sie Fat, F. E. (1983). Age metrics and twisted cylinders: Predictions from a structural model. *American Ethnologist, 10*(3), 585–604.

Tomson, P. R. V. (1985). Genograms in general practice. *Journal of the Royal Society of Medicine, 78*(8), 34–39.

Trotter, C. (2002). Worker skill and client outcome in child protection. *Child Abuse Review, 11*, 38–50.

Udry, R. J., & Hall, M. (1965). Marital role segregation and social networks in middle class, middle-aged couples. *Journal of Marriage and the Family, 27*(3), 392–395.

Usdansky, M. L. (2009, May). A weak embrace: Popular and scholarly descriptions of single-parent families, 1900–1998. *Journal of Marriage and Family, 71*, 209–225.

U.S. Census Bureau (2001). Survey of Income and Program Participation, Panel, Wave 2 http://www.census.gov/population/socdemo/marital-hist/p70–97/tab02.pdf. Accessed 19 May 2005.

Vanfraussen, K., Ponjaert-Kristoffersen, I., & Brewaeys, A. (2003). Family functioning in lesbian families created by donor insemination. *American Journal of Orthopsychiatry, 73*(1), 78–90.

Vaughan, P. (1989). *The monogamy myth: A new understanding of affairs and how to survive them*. New York: Newmarket Press.
Villeneuve-Gokalp, C. (2000). The double families of children of separated parents. *Population: An English Selection, 12,* 111–137.
Walker, A. (1997). *Elizabeth: The life of Elizabeth Taylor*. New York: Grove Press.
Warner, M. (2004). Beyond gay marriage. In D. Carlin & J. DiGrazia (Eds.), *Queer cultures* (pp. 768–782). Upper Saddle River: Pearson.
Wasserman, S., & Faust, K. (2009). *Social network analysis*. Cambridge: Cambridge University Press.
Waters, I., Watson, W., & Wetzel, W. (1994, February). Genograms: Practical tools for family physicians. *Canadian Family Physician, 40,* 282–287.
Weil, B. E., & Winter, R. (1993). *Adultery: The forgivable sin. Healing the inherited patterns of betrayal in your family*. New York: Carol.
Weinstein, D. (1992). Application of family therapy concepts in the treatment of lesbian and gay men. *Journal of Chemical and Dependency Treatment, 5*(1), 141–155.
Wellman, B. (1988). Structural analysis: From method and metaphor to theory and substance. In B. Wellman & S. D. Berkowitz (Eds.), *Social structures: A network approach*. New York: Cambridge University Press.
Werner-Lin, A. (2007). Danger zones: Risk perceptions of young women from families with hereditary breast and ovarian cancer. *Family Process, 46*(3), 335–349.
Westermark, E. (1994). Universal duty. In P. Singer (Ed.), *Ethics* (pp. 61–63). New York: Oxford University Press.
White, D. R. (2004). P-Graphs. *http://eclectic*.ss.uci.edu/~drwhite/pgraph/p-graphs.html. Accessed 5 Feb 2005.
White, D. R., & Jorion, P. (1992). Representing and computing kinship: A new approach. *Current Anthropology, 33*(4), 454–463.
White, D. R., & Reitz, K. P. (1983). Graph and semigroup homomorphisms on networks of relations. *Social Networks, 5,* 193–234.
White, D. R., Batagelj, V., & Mrvar, A. (1999). Analyzing large kinship and marriage networks with Pgraphs and Pajk. *Social Science Computer Review, 17,* 245–274.
Whitty, M. (2004). Cybercheating. *Counseling & Psychology Journal, 15*(8), 38–39.
Widmer, E. D., & La Farga, L. (1999). Boundedness and connectivity of contemporary families: A case study. *Connections, 22*(2), 30–36.
Wiemann, C., Agurcia, C., Rickert, V., Berenson, A., & Volk, R. (2006). Absent fathers as providers: Race/ethnic differences in support for adolescent mothers. Child & Adolescent Social Work Journal, 23(5/6), 617–634.
Wiggam, A. E., (1924). *The fruit of the family tree*. Garden City: Garden City Publishing.
Williams, B. K., Sawyer, S. C., & Wahlstrom, C. M. (2006). *Marriages, families and intimate relations*. Boston: Pearson.
Willow, R. A., Tobin, D. J., & Toner, S. (2009). Assessment of the use of spiritual genograms in counseling education. *Counseling and Values, 53,* 214–223.
Wilson, B. F., & Clarke, S. C. (1992). Remarriage: A demographic profile. *Journal of Family Issues, 13,* 123–141.
Wilson, R. J., & Watkins, J. J. (1990). *Graphs: An introductory approach*. New York: Wiley.
Winch, R. F. (1952). *The modern family*. New York: Henry Holt.
Winch, R. F., & Goodman, L. W. (1968). *Selected studies in marriage and the family*. New York: Holt Rinehart, and Winston.
Wolfe, A. W. (1978). The rise of network thinking in anthropology. *Social Networks, 1,* 53–64.
Worden, M. (2003). *Family therapy basics*. Pacific Grove: Brooks/Cole.

Author Index

D. Jedlicka, *Affinographs*, DOI 10.1007/978-1-4419-9395-3,

Subject Index

D. Jedlicka, *Affinographs*, DOI 10.1007/978-1-4419-9395-3,

Lightning Source UK Ltd.
Milton Keynes UK
UKOW030903170212

187415UK00004BB/1/P

9 781441 993946